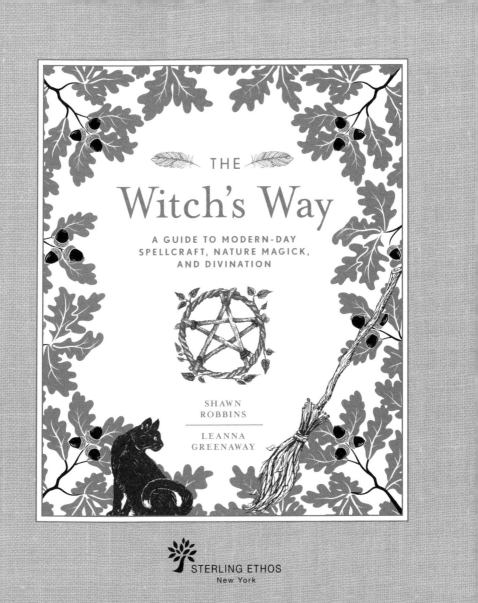

THE

Witch's Way

A GUIDE TO MODERN-DAY SPELLCRAFT, NATURE MAGICK, AND DIVINATION

SHAWN
ROBBINS

LEANNA
GREENAWAY

STERLING ETHOS
New York

STERLING ETHOS
New York
An Imprint of Sterling Publishing Co., Inc.

ISBN 978-1-4549-3082-2

For information about custom editions, special sales, and premium purchases,
please contact specialsales@unionsquareandco.com.

Printed in China

10 9

unionsquareandco.com

Interior design by Sharon Jacobs
Cover design by Elizabeth Mihaltse Lindy
Picture credits – *see page 303*

Dedicated to the never-ending journey,
illuminated by 1,001 magickal lights.
—*Shawn Robbins*

I dedicate this book to my lovely Dad,
who always said that I could achieve
anything I wanted if I put my mind to it.
This book is for you Dad.
—*Leanna Greenaway*

Contents

Part One: Wicca and Magick

Part Two: Spiritual Magick

Part Three: Divination Magick

Appendix

Authors' Notes

LEANNA GREENAWAY

In my opinion, if a faith feels right deep inside your soul, then believe it, and if it doesn't, then don't! Each one of us is unique, and we all must go through life at our own pace. I have been a witch since I was a teenager, but even as a small child, I always felt a calling and the need to reach out to a higher power. At the age of nineteen, when I began researching and studying witchcraft, I realized that this was the path I had to take. When I finally "came out of the broom closet," it didn't go down well with all my family members, but it was something that I really couldn't deny myself. Over time, they realized this and, thankfully, came to accept it. Nowadays, I am head of my own coven, where, once a month, nine of us meet and cast spells together for the good of mankind. I also have my very own YouTube channel where I perform demonstrations on things magickal.

My message to all the budding witches out there is this: you will know deep in your heart if Wicca is for you. It starts with an intense fascination that will draw you in. Often, people who take an interest in the craft in this life have been witches or healers in another, so the things they learn from studying Wiccan books sometimes feels like a reminder of what they already know. For me, Wicca is the love of my life, and I can't imagine not being able to follow my true path.

SHAWN ROBBINS

I believe we live in a world of indefinite possibilities, where everything is an enigma and we are all unique in our search for individuality. To me, labels do not define who, or what, we are; they are just a gateway to realize the true meaning of life. As for my own thoughts and musings, the path that I have chosen is a road less traveled, filled with hills and valleys. I look upon my journey as a perpetual student in life, and the people that I have met along the way—including Margot Adler and Sybil Leek—have had a profound effect in shaping my views and thoughts, both as a friend and teacher.

As authors, we also believe that we who promote the Wiccan way have a responsibility to learn from our "peers from the past," who laid a foundation of writings and teachings to grow upon. This includes the likes of Aleister Crowley, Helena Blavatsky, Scott Cunningham, Raymond Buckland, Robert Graves, Éliphas Lévi, Stewart Farrar, Samuel Liddell MacGregor Mathers, Owen Davies, George Pickingill, and Gerald Gardner, just to name a few. These people greatly influenced modern Witchcraft.

Preface

WITCHCRAFT TODAY

BELL, BOOK, AND MAGICK

No one is really quite sure when witchcraft began, but from what we can gather, it probably originated when human beings first assembled together in groups and worshipped the sun, moon, and stars. Historical records show us that it stemmed from the ancient Greeks, Romans, Hebrews, and Egyptians. Other cultures believe that it started with the ancient Celts—a group of people dating as far back as 700 BCE.

Whatever its origin, it is safe to say that magick and all things supernatural have made appearances in most cultures since the beginning of time. Although witchcraft today has its roots in Paganism, it is fast becoming one of the most popular faiths of the modern day. Human beings are more sophisticated than ever before and look for sense and logic when we are seeking an inner truth. We might be able to argue the fundamental facts of the Bible or other religious teachings, but you cannot deny that there is a moon and a sun in the sky, medicinal plants in the soil, and nature all around us.

Wicca is a spiritual following. It is a versatile faith, allowing you to sculpt and shape it in a way to suit your needs. For a belief to matter, it must chime within your heart and ring a truth deep within your soul.

The nice thing about the craft is that some people will embrace it completely, whereas others will only take on parts of it; a select few may merge their practices with other religions, such as Christianity. Wiccans do not frown upon other faiths. Wicca is a personal journey for everyone willing to experience it, and you can give as much or as little as you like.

History tells us that many of our traditions today were born from the ancient Pagans. Annual holidays such as Christmas, Easter, and Halloween, were once referred to as the Sabbats, and all the customs that we participate in today, such as blowing out candles on a birthday cake and making a wish, started with the ancient Greeks. People would adorn a cake with candles, which symbolized the glow of the moon, and take them to temples as an offering to Artemis. It is thought that the candle smoke carried their prayers to the heavens. It's funny to think that we all perform this ritual year in and year out when we blow out the candles on our birthday cakes!

Like with most things, witchcraft has evolved across the ages. Nowadays, Wiccans are proud of their faith and always try to work with the greater good, but in days gone by, Wicca had a dark side. Sadly, this bad press clung to witchcraft. It is not until we really delve deep into the recent history of the craft that we see how most of the current-day prejudice is quite misconstrued.

The witch trials in England, which took place around 1645, are a good example of this. Witchfinder General Matthew Hopkins projected widespread panic across the United Kingdom, and many innocent people were accused of working for the Devil, tortured, and often put to death.

Hopkins was a feared and evil witch hunter who worked with his associate, John Stearne, to line his own pockets. He swept across East Anglia and later traveled farther afield through Essex, trying and executing women for the crimes of witchcraft. Others accompanying him were employed to torture confessions of witchcraft out of the innocent victims. The accused would be submitted to sleep deprivation and be forced to stay awake for days, constantly walking around in circles until they were so exhausted, they had no other option but to confess. Another form of torture was cutting victims with a blunt knife. If a victim bled, she was proclaimed innocent; if she did not, she was sentenced to death for being a witch. One of Hopkins's preferred methods of torture was the swimming test. Accused women were bent double, tied up, and plunged into rivers and lakes. If they floated, they were condemned, and if they sank, they were innocent.

Hopkins became renowned across England for these practices and was paid a healthy fee of £23 from each town to rid them of their witches. This figure today would amount to approximately £4,000, so it seems that this was a lucrative career move for the witchfinder general.

Even today, people still shy away from the word witch and believe it to have some dealings with the devil. This couldn't be further from the truth. Witchcraft is not a form of Satanic worship like some would have you believe. Witches do not and never have believed in the Devil, because the Devil is a Christian concept.

Over the centuries people have advanced and, thankfully, so has witchcraft. Most Wiccans are gentle souls with good intent and a love of nature. They pride themselves on looking at the planet from a deeper perspective and becoming in tune with everything from a physical and spiritual standpoint. Like with any spiritual movement, there is good and bad, but it must be said that it is highly unusual for modern-day Wiccans to work with anything but good intent. More often than not, they will repel from becoming involved in anything other than what is right and pure. This is because Wiccans have a devout belief in that what goes around comes around, so if you do something cruel or unkind to another person, it is highly likely that your karma will catch up with you and something similar will befall you later down the line. Wiccans also have a code of ethics, which they stand by. The most upheld of these: harm none and do as ye will. Those adept in the craft believe entirely on a person's free will. They take their rituals very seriously and will always make sure that no one is affected negatively in the process.

This is the third book in the Modern-Day Witch Series, after *Wiccapedia* (written by the two of us) and *The Good Witch's Guide* (written by Shawn and Charity Bedell). In this book, we'll further explore different kinds of witches and what they practice; take a deeper look at cosmic helpers and more about how to work with them for a wide range of spells; and also cover all types of nature magic—from flowers to faeries. Plus there'll be a full-color chapter on pentacle power and comprehensive sections on divination, including using astrology and practicing botanomancy, the art of plant and herb divination. There is also a FAQs appendix on the most-asked questions about the craft.

Part One

WICCA AND
MAGICK

Chapter 1

Which Witch
are You?

MOST OF THE CURRENT RELIGIOUS MOVEMENTS ARE amalgamations of other, earlier doctrines, beginning with the first recorded imagery of ancient icons, including the all-powerful sun. Those who have an affinity for witchcraft often find themselves embarking on their own personal journeys. Unlike many other fixed religions, there are numerous varieties of witchcraft, all a little similar in one way or another but also with differences in the details.

Some people suppose that if you are a witch, then you are Wiccan, but this is not entirely true. Witchcraft is a faith where you must carve out your own path and find the route that rings true to your inner soul.

Your faith must be all about you; it is what the craft means to you as an individual and how you go about becoming at one with the universe and your surroundings.

Try to think of it as a way of creating yourself. So first, you must determine what being a witch means to you. It is far more than just owning a few crystals, saying the odd spell, or brewing some herbs to make tea. It is a way of life, a voice inside your head—a calling, if you like! If, as a small child, you were always drawn to things magickal, then you were probably born to be a witch. Whether you are a well-informed type or a beginner witch, there is always something new to learn.

Though all Wicca groups are based in British Traditional Wicca (BTW), over time Wicca has adopted a lot of offshoots that have developed and given birth to many new phases of the craft. For instance, Gerald Gardner became popular in the 1930s, when he brought witchcraft to the public's attention. He spent a lifetime trying to change the stigma associated with Wicca and became known as the father of witchcraft. As a result, he built a massive following across the world, which is now called Gardnerian Wicca, a New Forest branch of BTW.

Another example is Alexandrian Wicca, which was founded in the 1960s by English occultist and High Priest Alex Sanders. Gardnerian and Alexandrian Wicca are two well-known groups, but other smaller associations have broken away from the BTW and formed their own labels, creating new methods and traditions of their own.

We have a lot to thank Gardner for. He was instrumental in the birth of neo-pagan Wicca, reviving the wonderful, ancient art of witchcraft, and clearing the way for witches to practice freely today.

13 SIGNS YOU COULD BE
A NATURAL WITCH

1. **You have strange or prophetic dreams, often waking around the witching hour.**

   The witching hour is traditionally thought to be midnight, but many witches believe it begins around 3:00 a.m. It is important to pay attention to your dreams and keep a journal next to your bed to record your experiences during this hour.

2. **You have a rapport with nature and worry about the animal kingdom.**

   Witches have a likeness for nature, from the tiniest ant to the giant whales of the sea, and have an aversion to killing any living creature. Rather than step on them, they gently remove spiders and bugs from their houses and usually live with at least one pet.

3. **You feel an inner need to protect your planet and pay a great deal of attention to reducing your waste.**

   Witches are generally very "green," reusing bags and recycling anything they can. They have a fascination with the planet and respect all things living.

4. **You love to be outdoors and have a fondness for growing plants and herbs.**

   Whether it be in the ground or on the windowsill, there is an abundance of plant life budding all around you. You may also have an ardent interest in herbal remedies and medicines, often linking them to holistic therapy.

5. **You have a fascination with objects and believe they hold the power of luck, prosperity, or even protection.**
   You call them "lucky charms," amulets, or talismans and won't pursue important events without them at hand.

6. **You have heightened intuition.**
   Witches tend to walk into a room and almost immediately pick up on the atmosphere. Perhaps you can often intuitively tell if something is wrong with the people around you. This stems from being able to tap into the energy around a person. You may also experience feelings very deeply and be sensitive to your surroundings.

7. **You have an interest in one kind of animal, be it a cat, dog, spider, or crow.**
   Witches have been renowned for having "familiars" since the beginning of the craft. You may have a liking for a certain species of animal. Perhaps you already have a treasured cat, dog, or bird as a pet.

8. **The universe and solar system will captivate your interest, and you might believe life exists elsewhere.**
   Where a witch is concerned, there is no one set way of thinking. You like to be open-minded to all kinds of theories. An attraction to the universe and life on other planets enthralls you.

9. **You are a moral and upstanding person, always believing in the greater good.**

   There is a devout belief in Wicca that what goes around comes around, and because of this, a witch will never intentionally do anything to upset their karma. If you identify with this, then doing a nice thing for someone every day may be a common practice of yours.

10. **Faeries and other mythical creatures enchant you.**

    A witch's home is usually adorned with mystical items and ornaments. Because many witches believe in parallel realms, you may often sit quietly in wooded areas to breathe in nature and see if you can connect with nature spirits.

11. **You believe in the power of the spiritual world.**

    As a witch, you always believe that you are being helped spiritually and that someone in the spirit world is looking out for you, be it a lost loved one or a higher being.

12. **You like nothing more than being creative.**

    Any creative activity, such as arts and crafts, writing, or drawing and painting pleases you. Food and crafting with flavors and herbs is also important to many a witch.

13. **You have an avid interest in the supernatural and divination.**

    Not all witches are psychic, but many of them like to indulge in reading tarot or tea leaves. If you identify with this, then perhaps pendulums or even divining rods are present in your toolbox.

ALL MANNER OF WITCHERY

If you feel an inner witch calling to you, then it's time to embrace them. It is not imperative that you fall into any one category. Along the way, you might research many different forms of witchcraft before you settle on a method of belief that suits you. On the other hand, you could be more of an eclectic witch, using lots of varying methods in your craft. The choice is yours; this is your life and your faith.

With so many different types of witch out there, we've listed some of the most common groups practicing across the world today. See if you identify with any one of them.

So Which Witch Are You?

ALEXANDRIAN WITCH Following the established practices of Alex Sanders, these witches believe in the freedom of all witches and therefore, all other forms of witchcraft. Their focus is mainly on traditional methods of the craft.

ANGELIC WITCH This is a fast-growing, modern approach to witchcraft becoming popular in the UK and Europe. Angelic witches connect to universal vibration, replacing the traditional god and goddess used in rituals and spellcasting with angels. Their altars are often decorated with angelic representations, such as feathers, ornaments, and angel cards. They believe not just in a divine source but also in a celestial one. Because they trust solely in the power of the mind, they incorporate cosmic ordering alongside their spells.

BLOOD WITCH Also called hereditary witches, blood witches are people who have learned the craft from family members. They usually follow the "old" ways, which will have been passed down through the generations.

CELTIC WITCH This witch uses magickal practices that derive from the Celtic culture, following local folklore and, again, the "old" ways. However, Celtic witches do employ many basic and traditional forms of Wicca in their workings.

DRUID WITCH Commonly referred to as druidism, this practice worships nature and spirits and works in harmony to create a better environment, both spiritually and materially. This form of the craft has a large following, and it is thought that no two druids walk the same set path. Some honor the gods, whereas others have no religious intent. They use herbs to heal and divining methods to predict future events. Forest druids will sometimes respect Celtic forms of witchcraft.

ECLECTIC WITCH This witch needs a faith that speaks to their soul and so will pick and choose different parts of the many variations of witchcraft to suit them. They will not follow strict or set rules, allowing themselves to go with what feels right. Often, they follow their own chosen path. They borrow from all kinds of pagan or neo-pagan practices and utilize them into their own personal belief system. These can be from all four corners of the globe and covering many cultures. Often these witches reinvent some of the ancient pagan or Wiccan rituals into a more modern, functioning form of witchcraft, using similar tools but with an up-to-date twist. Eclectic Wicca is fast becoming the most commonly practiced in the field of witchery.

GARDNERIAN WITCH This subgroup follows the teachings of Gerald Gardner, specifically in the practice of neopagan Wicca.

HEDGE WITCH The term hedge witch stems from ancient times, when people lived in villages near forests or woodlands. The forest or woodland perimeters were called "hedges." They have a love of all things nature-based and use a variety of wild plants in their magickal rituals. This witch tends to lean toward spiritual workings. Meditation, healing, and lucid dreaming are all part of their craft. Like the solitary witch, they often cast spells alone, but many are joining online covens and sharing their knowledge with others. In years gone by, the hedge witch would be the person you sought out for healing a minor ailment. They have a wide knowledge of medicinal herbs and plants and blend their own remedies by the light of the moon.

GREEN WITCH Made popular by Ann Moura, this is an earth-based type of witchcraft, where the witch worships nature spirits and Mother Earth. Like hedge witches, green witches are very efficient with herbal remedies and are super proficient in the growing of plants. Chosen deities vary from witch to witch, but above all, they admire and respect the earth and the universe. Many green witches like to use the energies within natural objects such as stones, crystals, and the four elements: earth, air, fire, and water. Some have been known to practice ancient folk customs and traditional magick.

KITCHEN WITCH Kitchen witches—also sometimes referred to as cottage or hearth witches—use their homes and hearths as the primary focus for their craft. They are usually excellent cooks and delight in concocting delicious meals. They are renowned for infusing magick with their meals and using edible ingredients and potions as part of their rituals. When preparing food, a kitchen witch chants and stirs, kneads bread while reciting incantations, and projects their intent while summoning the energy within. They also incorporate magick while doing daily chores, such as sweeping away negative energies with a besom (broom) or using scented herbs and oils with their laundry.

LUNAR WITCH This subgroup of witch honors the moon and uses its influence in all their spells and rituals. They not only favor the lunar cycle in a magickal sense but also live their life by the phases of the moon, planning events and working each moon phase into everyday life. If this witch also follows a Hedgewitch tradition, you might find them using Farmers' Almanac to grow crops, planting and harvesting under the correct phases of the moon.

SECULAR WITCH This witch does not use any deities in their craft and often does not even work with anything connected to the supernatural. They can sometimes accept universal energy but choose not to connect witchcraft with religion.

SHAMANIC WITCH Some people argue that there is no association between witchcraft and shamanism, but Europeans do have their own type of shamanic faith. There are numerous forms of shamanism throughout the world. Most include a devout belief in the spirits, both good and bad, and seek to communicate with them. This is achieved via self-hypnotism, a trance-like state enhanced by drums and dancing, to achieve a certain level of consciousness. Healing is a major player, as is medicinal knowledge using plants and herbs. This practice is fast-growing throughout the western world and takes its roots from ancient beliefs.

SOLITARY WITCH A solitary witch is one who practices the craft on their own. In previous years, witches were loath to reveal their faith to anyone and kept their beliefs and rituals secret. Nowadays, because Wicca is more widely accepted, solitary witches have "come out of the broom closet," and although they still tend to practice in a solitary fashion, they discuss their magickal intentions with other like-minded people.

TEA WITCH These witches are often seen at the kitchen table, predicting the future by reading tea leaves. They also use tea as a kind of potion, blending and infusing herbs to combat minor ailments.

WEATHER WITCH When the weather is at its worst, weather witches are outside, collecting rainwater or snow to use in their rituals. They pull on the energy of storms and lightning and are devoted to all kinds of nature and the elements.

Angels vs. Goddesses

As modern witches in the twenty-first century, we wholly respect ancient, traditional methods of witchery and appreciate that Wicca is so diverse and that we are all different. What suits one witch will not necessarily be the calling of another.

Some witches lean more toward the use of either angel energy or goddess energy in their magick. Witches identify with both angelic beings and deities and find comfort in asking them for help when practicing any form of magick. Who better to summon when practicing magick than these wonderful beings?

Witches may have a personal affinity toward the angelic, but when you break it down, who is to say that they are not summoning the same beings as those who worship gods and goddesses? Perhaps angels and deities are the same beings but just have been given different names. It's a theory, but whether you are inclined toward the ancient gods or are more drawn to angels, there really is no right or wrong way to worship. If you have an attraction with one set of beings over another, then you must follow your heart. Each witch is at a different stage of spiritual evolvement.

Because we, the authors of *The Witch's Way*, see ourselves as eclectic witches, we sometimes pull on the power of a god or goddess during spellcastings, especially when practicing a ritual from an old spell book. We believe in the power of the goddess just as we believe in the influence of angels, and because we enjoy exploring all parts of the craft, we have no compunction in using both. Some traditional witches may not favor this method, but it works for us!

Goddesses

The sole roots of Wicca derive from human civilization itself, and when we look back at the earliest methods of witchcraft, we see that people of that time revered and worshipped the gods and goddesses. So many are used in magick, and all have their own influence and use in rituals to impact varying situations. Even today, thousands of traditional practitioners identify with their faith through a love of these ancient deities. We know for a fact that god and goddess worship predates Christianity, with ancient texts and cave drawings dating back to over 3,200 BCE. Isis was the supposed Egyptian goddess of magick and is often used in modern-day rituals by witches. Just as there are thousands of different cultures and beliefs across the world, there are thousands of deities to worship.

Below are some of the more commonly used angels and goddesses in magickal practices today.

APHRODITE Greek goddess representing beauty, love, and pleasure; her Roman counterpart is Venus, and she is identified with the planet Venus; included in rituals for finding your inner beauty, love and marriage, and romance

ARTEMIS Greek goddess of virginity and childbirth; her Roman counterpart, Diana, is goddess of the hunt; often connected with the moon; included in rituals for conception and easy childbirth

ATHENA Symbolizes wisdom, protection, and wars; her Roman counterpart is Minerva, goddess of wisdom and warfare, and is used in rituals for encouraging education and stopping upsets; Athena is included in rituals for gaining wisdom, for protection, and for warring families or neighbors

BRIGID Goddess of creativity, poetry, and crafts; included in rituals for inner creativity, writing, and painting or art

CERRIDWEN Goddess of prophecy; included in rituals for unleashing psychic abilities, divination, and foretelling the future

DEMETER Greek goddess of the harvest; sometimes called the Triple or Mother Goddess; included in rituals for lunar and garden magick, good harvests, and growing healthy plants and herbs

FORTUNA Roman goddess of wealth and fortune; included in rituals for boosting cash flow and for business and material wealth

FRIGG Norse goddess of household management and matrimony; included in rituals for manage-ment and organization around the home and for healing rifts in marriages and relationships

HATHOR Considered an important deity in ancient Egypt who embodied principles of love, motherhood, and joy; included in rituals for summoning strength and perseverance for new mothers and for bringing happiness into the home

HECATE Greek goddess of magick and witchcraft; often summoned to help enhance magick in spells; included in rituals for preparation magick

HESTIA Greek goddess of domestic situations; included in rituals for bringing about harmony in families and creating contentment in the home

ISIS Goddess of magick, creativity, and to strengthen the underdog; ncluded in rituals for enhancing magick in spells, to stop bullying, and for centering on inner creativity

JUNO Roman queen of the gods; goddess of matrimony; included in rituals for marriage and relationships

KALI Hindu goddess of time and death; included in rituals for aiding the passing of spirits to other realms and for protection in all things

LUNA Roman goddess of the moon; used by lunar witches to draw down the moon's power before rituals

MA'AT Egyptian goddess of truth and justice; included in rituals for anything legal, such as bringing about a positive legal outcome, and for seeking the truth from individuals

ROSMERTA Celtic and Roman goddess of abundance; included in rituals for success in business, for attracting more money, and for fertility and conception

SARASWATI Hindu goddess of education; included in rituals for concentration when taking exams and for any kind of education issue

SOL Norse sun goddess; included in rituals for drawing on the sun's power in spellcasting

UMA Hindu goddess of power, beauty, light, and wisdom; included in rituals for feminine empowerment, finding the answers to questions, and bringing in new things

Angels

Angels originally existed in Judaism, predating the start of Christianity. They were agents of God who fought the war between light and dark. Throughout time, angels have been given many different names to describe them. Some even believe that the Egyptian goddess Isis originally had a winged appearance when she arose in the form of an angel.

Today angels are recognized in many faiths, and millions of these beautiful beings can be summoned through prayer or ritual. Angels don't care what religion you practice; they only care that we spend time trying to perfect our souls and return to the one universal source that resides over everything.

If you are not sure which is the correct angel to summon when spellcasting, simply direct your incantations to "the angels." You can say something like, *"I summon the angel of abundance to aid me in my magickal workings"* or *"I call upon the angel of love and romance to assist me in my spell."* The angels will know who is right to support you and will send him or her along to help.

Here are some of the most commonly used angels that modern witches call upon in their magickal circles:

ARIEL Archangel of animals and the environment; included in rituals for anything pertaining to animals, wildlife, garden magick, and nature, and for planetary peace

AZRAEL Archangel of death; greets souls at the point of death and transports them to the spirit world; included in rituals for easing the transition from life to death and for help during the grieving process

CHAMUEL Archangel who provides strength and courage at times of adversity. Rituals for: Finding inner strength for life's hard lessons. Standing up to people who are controlling or overpowering. Finding lost objects, and moving to a new home

GABRIEL The archangel messenger of all angels who helps one overcome fear; also widely used with issues relating to children, conception, and birth; included in rituals for finding answers to questions, overcoming fearful situations, protecting a child when they are away, stopping a child from being bullied, or anything child-related

HANIEL Archangel of joy; included in rituals for romance, finding happiness and fulfillment, and easing frustration and disappointment

JEREMIEL Archangel of dreams and visions; included in rituals for physical development, prophetic dreams, meditation and visualization, and astral projection

METATRON Archangel of motivation and positive change; included in rituals for bringing about changes in life, moving to a new house, starting a new job, summoning motivation to succeed, and making any changes for the better

MICHAEL Archangel of defense and protection; is thought to be the most respected of all the angels; best called on in times of emergency or crisis; included in rituals for emergency situations, immediate help, protection from danger, removing negativity from a person or a residence, and banishing evil

RAPHAEL Archangel of emotional and physical healing; included in rituals for healing ailments, calming emotions, and easing depression, for any health-related matters, for help with the grieving process, and for boosting willpower

URIEL Archangel of wisdom and salvation; often helps spark the imagination; included in rituals for helping a person focus on the task at hand, bringing inspiration with a creative influence, and connecting with a higher power

Whether you are a gods-and-goddesses-type witch, are more comfortable asking the assistance of an angel, there is no right or wrong way to ask for help. Listen and tune in to your inner voice. Make the magick happen for you!

BASICS OF SPELLCASTING

Whichever form of witchcraft you decide to follow, most books state that some preparations must be undergone before commencing with any magick. For instance, casting a circle, setting up candles, and even the ways in which you speak can all influence your craft. But what exactly are these things for, and how can you prepare properly? Read on for helpful explanations.

Casting a Circle

The casting of a circle is vital to ensure your own protection when invoking energy of any kind. The circle acts as a forcefield of good, blocking out any negative energies that might otherwise enter your space. The circle also magnifies your own magick, encapsulating the power you are summoning.

Witches cast circles in many ways. Once again, this is personal to each practitioner, so add your own spin if you want. For those who have never cast a circle before, here is one method we use:

1. Find a flat, open space in your home, somewhere near your altar. The area doesn't have to be big—just large enough for you to stand inside.

2. Use a compass or your smartphone and find the four cardinal directions. Find one item that represents each of the elements. At each point in the circle, place the appropriate item on the ground.

For example:

> • **EAST** Represents air; possible items include dried sage or a sage smudging stick, a feather, or an incense stick
>
> • **SOUTH** Represents fire; possible items include an oil burner, a candle, or a tealight
>
> • **WEST** Represents water; possible items include a seashell, a small pot of sand, a chalice of water, or rainwater collected in a cup
>
> • **NORTH** Represents earth; possible items include a pot of soil, a potted plant, crystals, rocks, or stones

3. Stand in the center of the circle and face east. Relax your shoulders and visualize open air. Say these words: *"Spirits of air, I summon you."*

Turn to the south and imagine a candle flickering in your mind's eye. Say these words: *"Spirits of fire, I summon you."*

Turn to the west and envisage yourself on a beach, looking out to the ocean. Say these words: *"Spirits of the water, I summon you."*

Finally, turn to the north and picture yourself beneath a large oak tree with your hands on the ground.

Say these words. *"Spirits of the earth, I summon you."*

4. Remain facing north. Conjure up an image in your mind of all four elements shining a light to a focal point above your head. Hold this image in your mind's eye for a few minutes. Say these words:

*"Mother Earth, I thank you for your blessings
and ask that you fill this circle with luminous light.
Let nothing negative enter this space."*

The circle is now blessed.

"So mote it be."

Using Spell Candles*

These days witches use small, cigar-size candles for their spells, approximately 5 inches (13 cm) high. These are easily accessible online and can often be purchased directly from witches who choose to make their own. To prepare your candle, place it under running water to cleanse it and anoint it by smearing it with a small amount of pure vegetable oil.

* Never leave a lit candle unattended.

To Rhyme or Not to Rhyme

All spells are individual, and although there are thousands of spells in circulation today, there really is no right or wrong way to say them. Some spells rhyme while others do not. It's not all about having the perfect wording but more about the inner desire to reach your goal.

If you fancy yourself a poet or writer, you could try writing some of your own spells. The magick comes from deep inside the spellcaster, so the "intent" holds a power all its own. Just study which angel or god/goddess is appropriate for the task at hand and then investigate which crystals or herbs might best influence the subject. You often may find yourself up against a life problem not listed in a spell book. In such cases, you might not have any choice but to adopt and adjust an already-existing incantation or write a spell of your own. Some witches don't use tools such as candles and herbs at all but just have the confidence within themselves to project a thought or verse to acquire their need. Don't be afraid to experiment and test out lots of different ways to spellcast.

The most important factor in spellcasting is to believe in your own power and have no doubt in your mind that your incantation will work. Even the slightest uncertainty will cause failure, so it's vital that, before you start, you feel firm in your faith and are sure of your success.

RITUALS USING THE GODS, GODDESSES, AND ANGELS

Below are some examples of spells using corresponding items and different deities.

An Opening Ritual to Evoke the Goddesses

Once you have cast your circle and before you begin to cast your spell, it is important to invoke Hecate, the goddess of magick and witchcraft. She will bring about a peaceful ambiance and balance the energies around you. Perform this pre-ritual every time you cast a spell.

Hecate's main corresponding colors are silver, white, and gold, so choose one or more appropriately colored candles and place them at the back of your altar. Position some salt, water, and crystals next to the candles. These are ideal, to represent the four elements. You might like to add extra objects to your workspace, such as earth, an athame (ceremonial dagger), or the symbol of a pentagram. It is entirely up to you. When you're ready, focus on the flames and recite this spell:

> *"Hecate, goddess of magick,*
> *I ask for you to shine down your divine light.*
> *Cleanse the energy of this space in preparation for my spell.*
> *Every part of my being is bathed in your light,*
> *and I am channeled with your excellence.*
> *So mote it be."*

Your workspace is now fully charged, blessed, and ready for the spell at hand.

A Spell for Inviting Happiness with a House Blessing

Materials

- 7 pastel-colored candles, in white, pink, pale blue, green, lavender, yellow and orange, and seven candleholders
- 7 12-inch (30-cm) lengths of baby ribbon, in colors corresponding to the candles
- 7 candleholders

RITUAL

On a new moon phase, wrap each length of ribbon around each of the seven candleholders and tie with a bow. Put the candles in the holders, making sure that they correspond with the ribbon colors. Position them on your altar. They do not have to be in any order of color; just place them nicely on the surface and light them.

Recite this spell twelve times:

> *"Encircle this home with all that is dear,*
> *Bless this house and all who dwell here,*
> *I summon your power to rest in these walls,*
> *Goddess Hestia, hear my calls."*

Let the candles burn down and then untie the ribbons and braid them. Keep them near a window. The magickal forces will continue to work.

A Spell for Boosting Wealth with Goddess Help

Materials

A few coins

A green candle, for money, and a candleholder

A piece of paper with your bank details on it or a bank statement

RITUAL

Wednesdays are the best day to cast spells for money, so in the evening, set up your altar with your candle in the center, the coins scattered around the base of the holder and your bank statement to the side. Light the candle and say this spell nine times:

> *"Goddess Fortuna, hear me this day,*
> *Boost my cash flow so that I may*
> *Pay my bills with grace and ease,*
> *And all my worries will be released."*

When you have said the spell nine times, close it with the words *"So mote it be."*

Leave the candle to burn down, and within a few weeks, your bank account will be healthier.

An Opening Ritual to Evoke the Angels

Just as with the ritual for evoking the goddess, cast your circle and prepare your candles (see pages 17–19). The best angel to summon when preparing an opening ritual is the Archangel Michael. He is the dedicated protector and will ensure that nothing negative enters your workspace.

A Spell for Improving Luck and Restoring Peace with the Angels

Materials

Dried chamomile in a bowl, for invoking serenity

A lavender-scented tealight candle,
    for peace and tranquility

A piece of celestite crystal, situated on top
    of the chamomile, for releasing stress

RITUAL

Light the candle and say this incantation seven times with intent:

> *"Archangel Haniel, angel of joy and happiness,*
> *I require your presence this day to clear*
> *away all negative feelings.*
> *I desire fulfillment and contentment in my life.*
> *Shower me with magickal rays and give me*
> *the gift of life's pleasures."*

After you have said the incantation seven times, close the spell by saying,
"So mote it be."

Allow the candle to burn down. The celestite crystal now holds the power to leave you with feelings of happiness, so keep it nearby always and hold it at least once a day for five minutes.

A Spell for Angelic Help in Selling or Moving House

Materials

A small yellow candle, for the sun

A small blue candle, for house moves

A small piece of citrine crystal, for removing obstacles

RITUAL

On a new moon phase, lay your piece of citrine in the center of your altar and light both candles on either side of it. Say this incantation seven times:

> *"Archangel Metatron, prince of all angels,*
> *Manifest yourself here today and aid me in my magickal workings.*
> *Allow all blocks to be lifted out of the way so that*
> *I might dwell in a new residence.*
> *I call upon your divine light to assist me in this magick."*

When you have said the spell seven times, close the ritual by adding,
"So mote it be."

When the candles have burned down, bury the citrine somewhere outside, either in your garden or in a plant pot outside of the property.

Chapter 2

Draw Down the Moon

THE TOPIC OF LUNAR MAGICK HAS BEEN COVERED in another book in the Modern-Day Witch series: *Wiccapedia: A Modern-Day White Witch's Guide*. But just in case you never got around to reading it, here are some facts and helpful information if you want your lunar magick to be successful.

Often depicted as flying over it, witches love the moon. Each lunar phase throws out its own energy, so witches plan and arrange their rituals to fit with the lunar calendar. Practitioners of Wicca always advocate that a witch works from within and trusts their own instincts when casting spells and weaving magick. When it comes to discussing the moon and how it works, however, only studying will suffice.

PHASES OF THE MOON

Working in tandem with the phases of the moon is so very important. It is advisable that you study and ascertain what each phase is for, or, if you have a poor memory, make a note of them in your personal Book of Shadows so that you can refer to it quickly when you need information.

Full Moon

The full moon can affect emotions, and love spells tend to be favored during this phase, especially if it takes place on a Friday evening. This is a powerful time, when the moon radiates everything pertaining to romance and relationships. This is also a time to perform rituals for anything creative, because the full moon is somewhat mysterious. If you want to write fluently, paint beautifully, or play a musical instrument well, this is the phase for you.

CAST SPELLS FOR:

- Creating harmony in relationships
- Bringing peace into a marriage
- Prophecy and divination
- Stopping arguments between lovers or friends
- Bringing about a new romance
- Unleashing musical talents
- Removing psychic blocks
- Protection of home and property
- Emotional healing

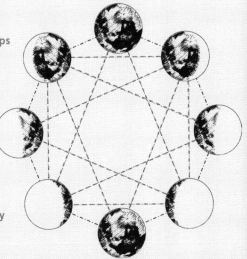

- General spells for luck
- Advancement of career or work
- Boosting self-confidence
- Any part of your life that needs extra power

Waxing Moon

This is a time for improving life and removing obstacles and blockages that stand in the way of progress. If you ever feel like you are in a rut or that significant oncoming changes are not happening quickly enough, then spells and rituals performed during the waxing moon will leave the way clear for moving forward. Anything associated with work, animals, or health-related issues will be successful. This is a positive moon phase, which usually helps solve problems and bring about desired results.

CAST SPELLS FOR:

- Issues or problems at work
- Healing and health difficulties
- Healing animals
- Money problems or spells to bring in more cash
- Helping a business to grow
- Removing mental blocks in education
- Passing exams
- Starting diets or breaking bad habits

- Moving to a new house or dealings with real estate
- Growth
- Beginning new projects
- Finding lost property

Waning Moon

A waning moon is a wonderful phase for eradicating anything that may be causing problems. The most appropriate spells to cast at this time are those that solve unwanted situations, such as harassment or issues with self-esteem. With the waning moon we can finally begin to take control of our lives and improve our inner strength, working on assertiveness and facing fears.

CAST SPELLS FOR:
- Removing negative vibrations
- Blessing houses and clearing away negative energies
- Banishing enemies
- Stopping harassment in the workplace
- Standing up to bullies and stopping intimidation
- Bolstering courage to stand strong
- Increasing willpower and determination
- Increasing assertiveness
- Banish evil influences
- Calming anxieties

New Moon

This is a time to bring about a new beginning, casting off the old and bringing in the new. You can use this phase for literally anything that relates to change. Ordinarily a waning moon is a good time to rid yourself of an unwanted situation, but once the moon changes into the new phase, you can cast a spell to bring about a positive replacement.

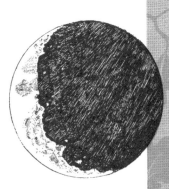

CAST SPELLS FOR:

- Starting a new diet
- Conceiving a child
- Bringing about a positive result in legal matters
- Getting a new job or winning a promotion
- Passing a driving test
- Bringing about new love or romance
- Getting married (always a nice phase in which to tie the knot)
- Changing a financial situation from bad to good
- Planning a nice holiday
- Travel, overseas or inland
- Moving to a new house or dealings with real estate
- Communication
- Better health

Dark of the Moon

This extremely powerful phase takes place at the tail end of a waning moon and shortly before a new moon, when the surface is almost completely cloaked in darkness. In the past, it was thought that those working with black magick or the darker forces would cast their spells at this time. There is no actual evidence of this, but to guard against anything negative, many witches avoid performing any rituals during the dark of the moon. If you are experienced in magick and want to bypass this tradition, you could try casting spells for the following.

CAST SPELLS FOR:

- Removing entities from houses or properties
- Banishing illness
- Divination
- Meditation and psychic visions
- Bringing about calm and peaceful results
- Conquering anger
- Bringing about justice

CALLING DOWN THE MOON'S POWER

Calling or "drawing down" the moon is a pleasing ritual you can perform to engulf yourself within the light of the divine essence. Many witches who cast spells frequently draw on the moon's power before every ritual. Some, however, only do it once a month, usually when the moon is in its full phase. The entire point of drawing down the moon is to connect with its powerful rays. You are permitting it to join you in your moment and work its magick alongside you.

While it is preferable to perform lunar magick outdoors, you might not want to be spotted acting oddly in your garden and thereby cause a scandal in the neighborhood. Being indoors or outdoors really doesn't make a lot of difference in the outcome of the spell, because you will still receive power from the divine light.

You can choose to perform this ritual prior to any spell, only once at the beginning of a new moon phase, or simply when you feel the need for some lunar cleansing. A lot of witches report a feeling of pure harmony afterward, both in mind and body, and the more sensitive witch might even feel quite emotional. Some have even reported that the entire experience was so moving, they cried.

There are many rituals to draw down the moon, but this one should leave you feeling invigorated, cleansed, and in tune with the divine.

Ritual to Draw Down the Moon

Materials

 1 (26-ounce) container of salt

 Wand or twig

 Chair or stool (optional)

RITUAL

For those more adventurous witches, you might like to go to the great outdoors. Your backyard, woodland areas, or open spaces such as fields are great places to conduct this ceremony. The important part is being able to see the moon in all its glory.

Playing peaceful, meditative music is also a lovely way to get into the spirit of the spell. Either way, be it indoors or out, the ritual is still the same.

Take a fair amount of salt and create a large circle with it on the ground. Step to the side and stand with your legs slightly apart. If you own a wand, point it at the moon. (If you don't have one, you can collect a large-enough twig from a nearby tree. Just be sure to thank the tree for its offering.) At this stage, gaze upon the moon's surface and imagine it radiating magick down from the skies. For a few minutes, breathe in its essence and visualize it showering you with magickal beams of light. As you inhale, picture yourself receiving power, and as you exhale, imagine you are breathing out any impurities in your body.

Say this spell three times:

"I call the goddess of the moon,
Bring your power around me and into my sight,
Silver light, shine down bright this night,
Fill me with your magick soon."

When you have said the spell three times, close it by saying, *"So mote it be."*

If you are fit and able, sit cross-legged inside your circle of salt and close your eyes. If not, sit on a chair or stool.

Hold the wand with both hands at each tip, top and bottom, and meditate on it. You might start to feel the wand become heavy with power, or you may feel a tingling sensation run up each arm. If this happens, it is a sign that the moon's magick is transporting its energy toward you. Completely relax your body, letting your head drop to your chin. Feel the stretch at the back of your neck, and hold this position for about ten seconds. Bring the head upward, this time turning it the right. Once again, hold for ten seconds. Repeat this, facing the left. Then, facing straight ahead, push back your shoulders for a further ten seconds before relaxing. Try to stay in this place for as long a period as you can. The more time you remain fully undisturbed and at one with your wand, the more the divine light will engulf you.

Some witches will use the lunar calendar every time they arrange an event in their life or cast a spell. Symbols of lunar animals, such as hares and badgers, are often present in a witch's home or on their altar. These creatures are steeped in magickal influence and represent the moon's presence during a ritual. It is also not uncommon for witches to wear moonstone jewelry or pendants decorated with the triple moon, representing Demeter, the Triple Goddess or Mother Goddess. The triple moon is composed of a full moon with a waxing and waning moon positioned at either side. Sometimes the full moon portion is replaced with a pentagram symbol.

However you want to celebrate it, one thing is certain: nearly all witches feel some affinity with the moon and worship it in their own way.

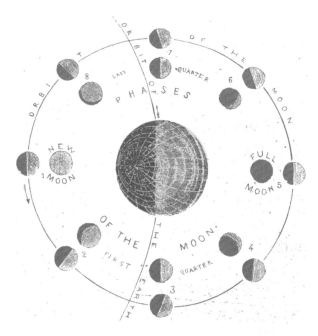

Chapter 3

Nature's Secrets

HAVE YOU EVER WONDERED WHY HUMAN BEINGS ARE naturally fascinated with all things relating to magick? Starting as small children, most of us have either read books on myth and legend or watched fairy-tale movies depicting witches, dragons, faeries, and the like. Folklore tells us that centuries ago, society truly believed in mythical creatures. We can argue that people of bygone times weren't as sophisticated as we are today and were far more likely to believe in fantasies, but their traditions have been around since the beginning of human culture. So do faeries, sprites, pixies, and leprechauns really exist, or are these just figments of our imagination, summoned by endless stories told through the ages?

Those of us with insight into the super-natural are often mocked or ridiculed, but if you think about it more logically, our universe is already unbelievable. We know very little about the planet we occupy and even less about the universe.

We are so wrapped up in our high-tech lives that we pay little or no attention to our real purpose here on Earth, and we often dismiss anything we don't fully understand. So why is it that the human race has paid so much attention to magick and myth? Could it be that faeries, pixies, and trolls truly live out there somewhere? Just because we don't fully understand it doesn't mean it's not true!

Where all people can physically see and feel the world around us, some of us believe many parallel realms sit directly alongside our earth realm. Those who are more fortunate can attune their consciousness so that they can actually *see* these parallel realms. Some have even described seeing elementals such as faeries, goblins, and woodland creatures in their gardens or spotting strange creatures in their vision's periphery when out walking in the woods. It may sound farfetched, but try to imagine a veil that separates these dimensions from our own. Witches believe that we live alongside multiple parallel realms without even knowing it.

If you have a love of all things mythical and would like to connect with the other realms, read on.

THE MAGICK OF MYSTICAL CREATURES

If you know anything about Wicca and witches, then you know that all living creatures are held in high regard. We think of all creatures, large or small, as purposeful, valuable, and worth protecting. And that includes creatures of myth and legend. Faeries, unicorns, and dryads are three such classes of creature. They, along with the staple Wiccan symbol the Green Man, encompass the knowledge held in this chapter.

Faeries

Faeries, also referred to as fairies, fae, fey folk, elves, dwarves, pixies, sprites, brownies, and gnombes, are thought to regularly flutter in and out of the realms, visiting and even residing here. Over time they have been seen by thousands across the world. You have probably seen a faerie before now and didn't even realize it. They can appear as tiny dashes of light twinkling around trees, and occasionally you might hear the faint sound of high-pitched bells.

Leanna's Perspective

Let's go ahead and dispel the myth: faeries do not appear as inch-high pretty girls with flowery dresses, long golden tresses, and wings.

Many summers ago, while sitting on my lawn, I believe I saw a faerie. I only caught sight of it for a few seconds as it ran straight down the path to the side of me. The creature was more alien-looking than anything human. It appeared as an illuminous, pale yellow haze in the form of a naked humanoid body, standing around eight inches (20 cm) tall. Its head was larger and more elongated than a human head would be, and it didn't have any hair. The wings were transparent, resembling a cobweb, and had a large span. I immediately recognized it as being a faerie. I blinked a couple of times to see if I could spot it again, but to no avail.

I can only think that, being in a peaceful, serene state, I was able to tap into another realm. Since that time, I have had a devout belief in nature spirits. I'm not entirely sure what their purpose is, but I know they exist.

Where You Can Find Faeries

These creatures are usually spotted in areas such as ponds, lakes, dense woodland, and under trees. Their preferred tree is said to be the flowering hawthorne, found on the British Isles. Folklore tells us that they are also attracted to circles of mushrooms, cleverly nicknamed *faerie* or *pixie rings*. These circular mushroom patches grow in lawns. They can also look like dark, round rings imposed on grass; these are called superficial pixie rings and occur where the fungus breaks down. They can also live beneath tree canopies or in a tree's grooved-out hollows.

These are all common places for faeries to dwell, but faeries are not always tied to the great outdoors. They can even live in your house! If a faerie is living nearby or even in your home, there are certain signs to look for.

Are Faeries Living Nearby?

- Wild plants may be growing around the property. They often poke out from the brickwork of any paths adjacent to the home.

- You might notice an influx of dandelions, as faeries enjoy blowing them in your direction.

- Your average pet can see faeries and nature sprites, so you may notice your dog or cat gazing sideways or looking at something that isn't visible to you. Their behavior can become skittish and playful.

- Birds might also perch on your window ledges briefly before flying away.

- Beware: faeries like to steal. Small, sparkly items, such as jewelry or coins, could go missing—and then turn up months later in a strange place.

- Small items of clothing, such as socks or ties, may vanish.

- A faint sweet smell might permeate the home.

Attract Faeries into Your Home

- Place a few plants around the home. Faeries particularly like fragrant plants, such as lavender.

- Open the windows every day to let in the sunshine and fresh air. Make sure your curtains don't block out the sunlight.

- Try to decorate your home in light shades—faeries do not like dark colors.

- Create a faerie ring made of pebbles, stones, and crystals in your garden. Place something sweet-smelling, such as cut flowers, in the center.

- Try to keep your mood happy. Faeries don't like it when you frown or shout.

- Have a faerie figurine or artwork placed somewhere in your house. This will make them feel welcome.

A Spell for Accessing Other Realms

This spell should be performed on the night of a full moon when the sky is clear.

RITUAL

On the night of a full moon phase, when the sky is clear, sit outside in the moonlight and gaze up at the moon. Place both hands on the ground and ask the universe to bathe you in magick. For around five minutes, close your eyes and imagine the light of the moon shining down on your head and face. Say these words three times:

> *"The magick I pull when the moon is full,*
> *Down to me so I can see,*
> *Nature sprites come this night,*
> *Show yourself, faerie and elf"*

Stay outside for a further five minutes before going indoors. Pay attention to the way you feel over the coming weeks and look for signs you might have missed before.

A Spell for Attracting Faeries

If you want to attract the fey folk to your home, try this spell during a
new moon phase.

Materials

> A white candle and candleholder
>
> A selection of crystal tumble stones, of
> your choosing
>
> 4 or more pebbles or stones from outside
> your home
>
> A sprig of lavender
>
> A sprig of heather

RITUAL

Put the candle on a table somewhere near your fireplace or in the focal point
of your home's primary lounge area. Place your crystals and pebbles or stones
in a circle around the candle. Situate the sprigs of lavender and heather in the
center of the stone circle, then say this spell seven times:

> *"Faeries, come and stay a while,*
> *For you are greeted with cheer and a smile,*
> *Settle here and make your home,*
> *And you shall never be alone."*

Leave the candle to burn down without blowing it out.

Unicorns

Lots of modern-day witches adore
unicorns. Their energy is thought to be
completely pure, so much so that legend
has it only a virgin hand can physically touch
a unicorn. Unicorns bring luck into the home
and fill it with lightness, protection, and innocence.
Place a picture of, or a small ornament of a white unicorn somewhere in
the home to protect the residence and all who dwell within it.

The Green Man

We cannot write this chapter and
have no mention of this wonderful
Wiccan icon. The Green Man
is a nature deity often depicted
through a sculpture or figurine
of a man's face encircled with
leaves, branches, and foliage. His
origin is believed to be Pagan,
but many countries and cultures
across the globe have their own adaptation. Often represented in the
form of a plaque or plate, he can be placed on the outer walls of a house,
overlooking the garden and all of the wildlife that resides nearby. His
main purpose is to protect animals and plants from harm. He sends out
positive, protective vibrations and can be found guarding the gardens of
most witches.

THE MAGICK OF TREES

A tree hugger is often thought of as eccentric and most likely scoffed at, but have you ever actually wrapped your arms around a large tree and stopped for a moment to feel the vibrations? I agree that there are many eccentric witches out there, but if you close your mind to the hustle and bustle of life just for a moment and take the time to embrace a tree, you will have one-on-one contact with the lungs of the earth. Their powerful roots are directly in tune with the earth's energy source, so if you stay in position and concentrate on this long enough, you will be sure to feel it.

I admit, I delight in hugging trees, eccentric or not. Besides, how can a person not believe in the influence of these incredible living organisms, especially when they are everywhere?

What many people don't know is that very large, old trees with fat, plump roots often house tree spirits called dryads. Sit beneath an oak or any other large tree. Do you feel anything? Their energies can often be felt by the more sensitive among us.

In ancient Greek mythology, as today, dryads, also called *spirits of nature* or *wood nymphs*, were thought to live in forests and groves, overseeing the woodland's plants and trees. These wood nymphs are often considered female, and each presides over a particular tree. Dryads are considered very shy, but be warned: they punish anyone who might hurt or harm a tree.

A Spell to Tap into Dryad Power

If you want to get as close to nature as possible, then try this spell.

On a dry day, venture out into a forest or wooded area, place a blanket on the ground beneath a large tree, and sit. Oak trees are best if you can find one. As you sit, look up at the branches above you and drink in the fresh air. Place your hands on the ground and stay still for a few minutes. Say this spell quietly to yourself while concentrating on the roots beneath your fingers:

> *"From the roots on the ground to your branches of strength,*
> *I attune your power, your magickal length,*
> *Spirits of nature, wood nymph, or dryad,*
> *Entwine with my energy, make my soul glad."*

When you have said the spell a few times, stand up and place your arms around the tree, feeling the magick of the dryad coursing through your veins. Quietly repeat the spell. The longer you stay near the tree, the more power you will receive. This spell is very good if you suffer from minor ailments, as a person is thought to receive healing strength from the tree.

Tree Properties and Their Magickal Influences

Literally every tree in the world has a magickal influence, so for those interested in this subject, I suggest you research them at length, but for now, here is a list of the most popular trees a witch might include in her rituals.

We have not discussed wands at length in this book, but just know that wands are thought to help direct a witch's power. Making a wand from any of the following woods will bring individual properties of that tree to the spell at hand. For other rituals, the fruits, leaves, or berries of a tree can be used to enhance a spell and incur a more successful result.

Before you remove even the smallest amount of bark, a leaf, or a bloom from a tree, it is important that you ask permission. Stand in front of the tree and touch the bark for a few minutes. The tree will read your mind, so tell it why you want its help. Once you have taken what you want from the tree and before going on your way, thank it.

ALMOND TREE (*Prunus dulcis*) Success in business; clairvoyance and enhanced psychic ability
Good for getting loans approved or increasing cash flow. Eat a small handful of almonds every day to increase your psychic flow and boost prosperity.

APPLE TREE (*Malus*) Healing disruptive love affairs, restoring harmony
Apple wood wands are used for anything to do with love, romance, harmony, and peace, and are used in magick to promote visions. Slice an apple in half one way and you will see the sign of a pentagram. Slice it the other way and you will see a likeness to female genitalia. For harmony, place a photo of you and your loved one between the two halves of an apple and secure with a skewer. Leave it overnight under the full moon, and your relationship will improve.

ASH TREE (*Fraxinus*) Communication, removing mental blocks, creativity
Place the leaves of an ash tree on your altar while conducting spells for the aforementioned concerns. When you have finished, always take the leaves back to where you found them.

BEECH TREE (*Fagus*) Healing, specifically for inflammatory issues
Find a large beech tree and stroke the branches, gently asking the nature spirits to send you healing.

BIRCH TREE (*Betula*) Change and fertility
Excellent for wand magick when spellcasting for fertility or calming emotions. To increase your chances of fertility, on the first day of a new moon phase, search the ground beneath a birch tree and collect the fallen leaves you find there. Place these leaves in a small pouch and put the pouch under your mattress. Make love on the bed every night until the moon begins to wax.

CEDAR TREE (*Cedrus*) Prosperity, Money Luck, and Increased Cash Flow
To increase cash flow, take a few sprigs of cedar and place them in a vase in your home. To improve your finances, take a tiny amount of bark and keep it in your wallet. Cedar wands, if you choose to use one, are beneficiary for clearing away negative energies in houses.

ELDER TREE (*Sambucus*) Healing and protection
Pick elderflowers when they are in full bloom to make a healing potion (lots of nice elderflower cordial recipes can be found online). When your cordial is made, light a yellow candle beside the liquid and, for a few minutes, visualize protective and healing light shining down through your head. Let the candle burn down until it extinguishes itself. Drink two small glasses of the elderflower potion every day.

FIG TREE (*Ficus*) Energy and strength
To boost your energy, collect a very small amount of earth from around the roots of a fig tree. Sprinkle it inside your shoes and leave overnight. The next morning, go outside and empty the soil from the shoes.

HAWTHORNE TREE (*Crataegus*) Marriage and reconciliation
To reconcile a troubled marriage, pick a handful of flowers or leaves from a hawthorne tree and take them home to dry. Once dry, place them in a bowl somewhere in your house. These trees are also particularly attractive to faeries.

LEMON TREE (*Citrus limon*) Chastity and divination
To ward off evil spirits, squeeze the juice of three lemons into a plastic spray bottle. Add three cloves. Shake well and spray around the entrances to your home.

MAPLE TREE (*Acer*) Love and romance
For all single people: attract the perfect partner by collecting a leaf from the maple tree in autumn. Press the leaf in a book for a few weeks. Once flattened, and during a full moon, place a pink candle on top of the leaf and light it. Let the candle burn down.

OAK TREE (*Quercus*) Money and vitality
The bark, leaves, and roots of the mighty oak tree possess magickal properties. Use them in spells to improve your vitality and attract money. This is also a great tree to hug if you are feeling unwell.

OLIVE TREE (*Olea europaea*) Fidelity
To keep your partner loyal, purchase a small olive tree. Keep it in a pot, either in a glass conservatory or on a sunny patio.

PEAR TREE (*Pyrus*) Longevity
In Chinese folklore, the pear tree possessed the power of immortality. Grow a pear tree in your garden for a long and healthy life.

ROWAN TREE (*Sorbus*) The witch's tree
Anyone interested in Wicca should have a rowan tree in their garden or nearby to access. The rowan is thought to bring divine protection to property and encourage wildlife in the surrounding area.

WILLOW TREE (*Salix*) Enchantments and good health
When made into a wand, willow wood is the very heart of magick and can be used to cast a circle before any spell commences. It can also give strength and wellbeing to the sick and the elderly.

THE MAGICK OF FLOWERS

Witches often like to place flowers on their altars to symbolize the spell at hand. These can be fresh but are often dried so a large portion can be bought and stored for future use. The petals are scattered upon the altar or around the candles used in the spell. Their significance can bring about a more successful result to the ritual's outcome. Because there are thousands of varieties the world over, it is not unusual for witches to keep a list of each flower and its magickal correspondence in their Book of Shadows. (See pages 282–83 for more on Books of Shadows.) Below is a list of the more common blooms we use in our practices today.

ACACIA (*Acacia*) To hide a secret love affair

APPLE BLOSSOM (*Malus domestica*) For luck and good fortune

BLUEBELL (*Hyacinthoides*) Used to attract faeries; stops nightmares when placed inside a pillowcase; promotes humility

BUTTERCUP (*Ranunculus L.*) Affects children and friendships

CARNATION (*Dianthus caryophyllus*) Used for love magick and removing hexes

CHAMOMILE (*Chamaemelum nobile*) Used for restful sleep, animal support, peace, and harmony

CHERRY BLOSSOM (*Prunus serrulate*) Used for romance and weight loss

CHRYSANTHEMUM (*Chrysanthemum indicum*) Used for mental clarity and healing from grief

CROCUS (*Crocus sativus*) Used for guarding the heart, cheerfulness

DAISY (*Bellis perennis*) Used to bless babies and for naming ceremonies and Wiccanings; symbolizes protection

DAFFODIL (*Narcissus*) Used for unrequited love

DANDELION (*Taraxacum officinale*) Used for animal protection and enhancing divination

ECHINACEA (*Echinacea purpurea*) Useful for anything pertaining to aiding health problems

FEVERFEW (*Tanacetum parthenium*) For problems pertaining to the head, headaches, migraines

FORGET-ME-NOT (*Myosotis*) Present in love spells and handfastings; improves memory and organization

GARLIC (*Allium sativum*) Wards off evil; protects the home and environment

HONEYSUCKLE (*Lonicera*) Fosters faithfulness, loyalty, and fidelity; awakens sexual pleasure.

HYACINTH (*Hyacinthus*) Attracts gifts and glamour

IRIS (*Iris*) Used for inner truth and clarity; attracts messages from spirits

JASMINE (*Jasminum*) Used for abundance, joy, and sexual healing

LAVENDER (*Lavandula officinalis*) Used for balance and harmony; improves sleep and anxiety; releases guilt

LILAC (*Syringa*) Used to strengthen power and balance chakras

MAGNOLIA (*Magnolia grandiflora*) Used for goddess energy and personal power

MARIGOLD (*Tagetes*) Used for detoxification, happiness, and healing depression

NASTURTIUM (*Tropaeolum*) Casts away fears of new situations

ORCHID (*Orchidaceae*) Used for wealth and luxury, sexual pleasure, romance, and heightened intuition

PANSY (*Viola tricolor var. hortensis*) Releases stress and attracts purity

PASSIONFLOWER (*Passiflora*) Removes anxiety and helps to alleviate pain in the body

PEONY (*Paeonia*) Used for exorcism, self-confidence, money, and success

PETUNIA (*Petunia*) Used for domestic bliss and fresh perspectives

POPPY (*Papaver somniferum*) Calms nerves, and helps one make peace with death

PRIMROSE (*Primula vulgaris*) Heals a broken heart and changes karma; used to increase outspokenness

ROSE (*Rosa*) Used for riches and wealth, blessings, emotional healing, and romantic love

SAGE BLOSSOM (*Salvia officinalis*) Clears away negativity; improves emotional disentanglement and self-respect

SWEET PEA (*Lathyrus odoratus*) Used for friendships and support

TULIP (*Tulipa*) Used for desires and wishes; improves love and romantic healing

VERBENA (*Verbena*) Used for work matters, physical healing, and magick

WATER HYSSOP (*Bacopa monnieri*) Also known as Indian pennywort, and when ground up, as Brahmi powder, it is used for relieving sadness and anxiety

WISTERIA (*Wisteria*) Heals grief, soothes stress, and improves wisdom

YLANG-YLANG (*Cananga odorata*) Used for relaxation and weight loss; improves body image

How to Use Plants, Bark, and Flowers in Your Spells

There are countless ways you can use nature's vegetation in your spells. Each living organism on the earth has a purpose. Human, animal, and plant life are all part of the cosmos, and we can pull on each vibrational energy to accomplish our desires. Most herbs and plant life contain healing properties, and it is thought that for every single ailment on the planet, there is a plant to combat and cure it. We just have to establish which one will do the job at hand.

Hedge witches, who we discussed in chapter 1, are often wonderful herbalists and will mix potions and medicines to combat some smaller health issues. But you don't have to be a hedge witch to utilize a plant's magickal correspondence or use it as a symbol on the altar. For example, we know that the plant feverfew is wonderful for healing migraines and headaches. Simply putting a few feverfew leaves in a sandwich or steeping it in a tea will reduce symptoms very quickly. We can also adapt its purpose and place a handful of the flowers or leaves, fresh or dried, on the altar to symbolize this or other problems pertaining to the head. Witchcraft doesn't come with hard-and-fast rules, so you can slightly modify any spell by including plants in your rituals.

Another example: We know lavender is good for releasing anxiety, so if you want to perform a spell to relieve stress, you could anoint your chosen candle with lavender oil or place a dried bunch of lavender somewhere on your altar. Of course, it would be even better if you infuse your own lavender oil by steeping a few sprigs of the herb in a small bottle of vegetable or olive oil, and then leaving it to steep for 24 hours to generate its magick. You can even grow the plant in your garden or on your windowsill. The magick a spell brings will be amplified with the correct items nearby.

Below are some general spells you can try with plants, bark, and flowers.

A Spell to Say Goodbye to Stress

Materials

A white candle, for purity, and a candleholder

Lavender essential oil, for releasing stress and anxiety

A small bowl of Brahmi powder, for increasing feelings of happiness

A bunch of dried lavender, for releasing stress and anxiety

RITUAL

Hold your candle for a few minutes and think back to a happy time in your life when there were no worries and you were truly contented. Next, to anoint the candle, dip your finger into the lavender oil. Run your fingers in a line from the top of the candle to the bottom. (See pages 266–68 for a list of essential oils and their uses.) Place the candle in a holder and sprinkle the Brahmi powder around the base. Position the bunch of lavender somewhere nearby and say this spell three times:

> *"Disconnect me from my stress,*
> *Fill the void with happiness,*
> *With this spell and magickal aids,*
> *From within, anxiety fades."*

When you have said the spell three times, close it by adding, *"So mote it be."*

Leave the candle to burn down without blowing it out. When it has extinguished itself, hang the lavender, facing downward, in a window. This will transport happiness through the house, which in turn will help your sense of wellbeing. The Brahmi powder will now be charged and blessed, so put it somewhere safe for use in future spells.

A Spell to Attract New Love

Materials

A length of pink satin ribbon, for love

A small sprig of cherry blossom or pink rose petals
in bloom, for romance

A handful of lovage root, for love and eroticism (see page 66)

A medium-size bowl

A pink candle, for love, and a candleholder

Rose essential oil, for love

RITUAL

On a Friday during a full moon phase, wrap the ribbon around the stem of the cherry blossom and tie with a bow. Place the lovage in the bowl and situate the cherry blossom on top. Anoint the candle, by dipping your finger into the rose oil. Run your fingers in a line from the top of the candle to the bottom, then place the candle in a holder. Say this spell seven times:

"Show your face, come into view,
So that I connect with you,
Hear my heart beat, feel my need,
Part of a couple I shall be."

When you have said the spell seven times,
close it by adding, *"So mote it be."*

When the candle has burned down, take the cherry blossom sprig or pink rose petals outside and place it on the ground. Scatter the lovage all around it. Touch the tree and silently ask it to grant your wish.

A Spell to Boost Cash Flow

Materials

A small amount of bark from an oak tree

2 drops juniper berry essential oil, for protecting finances

2 drops ginger root essential oil, for adding power to a spell

2 drops frankincense essential oil, for attracting wealth

A green candle, for money, and a candleholder

Dollar bill or other monetary note

A whole nutmeg, for attracting cash

RITUAL

A Wednesday during a waxing moon is probably
the best time to cast a spell for money. Find a
nearby oak tree and place both hands on the
trunk. Silently ask the tree to give you a piece of
bark for your spell. Break off a very small amount
and thank the oak for its offering. Back at home,
blend together the juniper berry, ginger root, and
frankincense essential oils. (See pages 266–68 for
a list of essential oils and their uses.) Anoint the candle,
by dipping your finger into the oil blend. Run your fingers in
a line from the top of the candle to the bottom, then place the candle
in a holder. If you have difficulty obtaining these oils, you can substitute pure
vegetable oil. The spell will work but will probably take a little longer.

During this waxing phase, set up a small altar somewhere in your home and
lay your dollar bill in the center. Situate the candle directly on the top and rest
the nutmeg and bark on either side. Say this spell once:

> *"With nutmeg and bark, I make my mark,*
> *Let magick flow and abundance grow,*
> *Richness and wealth come to me and line my pockets,*
> *So mote it be."*

Let the candle burn down on its own without blowing it out. After it has
extinguished itself, keep the nutmeg and bark in your coat pocket for at
least a month. Your cash flow will start to improve.

A Spell to Protect Your Garden's Wildlife

During the harsh winters, birds and wildlife often perish. It's important for a witch to help them not just survive in these cold months, but thrive.

Materials

> Three candles, in green, brown, and blue, for representation of nature's colors
>
> Three lengths of ribbon, in green, brown, and blue

RITUAL

Stand the three candles in the center of your workplace. It doesn't matter in which order you place them. Light them.

Take the three lengths of ribbon and knot them together at the top before braiding them into a plait. Fasten the plait at the bottom. Lay the braid in front of the candles and say this spell three times:

> *"Goddess of wildlife, discharge your power,*
> *Bring safety and contentment, hour upon hour,*
> *Treasure the animals who reside outside,*
> *Be their comfort, be their guide."*

When you have said the spell three times, close it by adding, *"So mote it be."*

Let the candles burn down. When they have extinguished themselves, go outside and tie the braid to a branch of any tree in your garden. Make sure you feed the birds and put out fresh water when the weather becomes harsh and make sure that if it freezes you break up or melt the ice so that the birds always have a drink. (We pour warm water on our icy bird baths in freezing conditions.)

For Friendship with Your Ex Through Divorce

Though divorce rates are on the decline, separations still occur and can be quite messy. Often little children are caught in the crossfire and can end up being used as pawns during divorce proceedings. I'm sure everyone undergoing divorce hopes their relationship with their ex remains amicable, especially where kids are involved. This spell will help wipe away the tension during this difficult time and remove the painful emotions that can cause spite and unkindness.

Materials

> 1 black candle, for stopping arguments,
>   and a candleholder
>
> 1 white candle, for protection and kindness,
>   and a candleholder
>
> Vegetable oil
>
> Pen and paper
>
> A handful of dried passionflower, for bringing
>   acceptance and peace to the heart
>
> A small bowl

RITUAL

On the first night of a new moon phase, begin by anointing both candles with pure vegetable oil. Write your ex's name on the piece of paper and lay it in the center of a small table. Position the candles on either side. Scatter the dried passionflower all around the paper and the base of the candles. Speak the following incantation nine times:

"I sense your dislike, I feel your spite,
I intend to challenge it on this night.
Your wrath will fade, your bitterness gone,
In the days to come, you shall harm none.
Acceptance and friendship, our manners mild,
As we go forward in raising our child."

When you have said the spell nine times, close it by adding, *"So mote it be."*

When the candles have burned down and extinguished themselves, gather up the dried passionflower and place it in the bowl. Leave the bowl somewhere in your house so its magick can infiltrate all around.

THE NATURAL WITCH'S TASK

Nothing saddens a witch more than people who disrespect our planet. All witches worship nature and respect every living thing, from a blade of grass or a tiny ant to the stars in the sky. Everything has a purpose, and every single living being is just as important as the next. By taking time each day to admire the wonder of our natural environment, you will raise your spiritual vibration and improve your soul.

Chapter 4

Poppets and Pouches

A POPPET, ALSO KNOWN AS A POPPIT, PIPPY, OR MOPPET, is a handmade doll created and used in spellcraft. These effigies are used to represent an individual and to aid the person through the use of magick. In folklore and across many cultures, poppets were used to both heal and harm and often contained something belonging to the targeted person, such as hair, toenail clippings, or tiny pieces of clothing. Some traditions forbid the use of poppets, seeing them as stereotypical voodoo dolls, but like with anything pertaining to the craft, it is all about intent. Many modern witches use them in gentle magick and only utilize their power with love and light in mind or to enhance and improve someone's life.

Traditionally poppets are made from wool, straw, carved roots, wax, paper, potatoes, or cloth, and material dolls were packed with all manner of items, ranging from trinkets to crystals to herbs. Basically you can use any material you like, but many believe that the more effort you put into making the doll, the greater your success will be in achieving your final goal.

In this chapter, we will discuss making poppets using easy-to-obtain items. You can be as imaginative as you like, but it is important to include the correct materials for the matter at hand. You can craft a doll that represents yourself, or, if you have a friend or family member in need of a little help, you can make an effigy strictly for them and cast the spell on their behalf.

THE MANY PARTS OF A POPPET

In this part of the chapter, we will show you how to easily make a poppet using fabric and herbs. You can add crystals or other items if you have knowledge of their significance.

Materials, Cloth Types, and Colors

You can use any kind of cloth capable of being stitched. Felt, cotton, wool, and linen are popular choices, but it really doesn't matter. If you are making a poppet for a loved one, you might like to cut up one of their old shirts to use. Later in this chapter you will learn about the importance of having something belonging to the individual. An item of clothing is a great idea!

Every color has a built-in energy field, which is why many witches use particular colors for certain goals. Here are the Wiccan meanings of colors:

BLACK Enhances a person's wisdom; safety when out and about, protection in general; banishing someone from your life; hex reversal

BROWN Blessing a house; anything relating to animals and pets; locating lost objects; improving concentration; moving or selling houses, real estate

DARK BLUE Forgiveness; good fortune; willpower and weight loss; astral projection; fidelity; domestic bliss

DARK YELLOW OR COPPER Success in business; climbing the career ladder; money

GREEN Boosting money energy; emotional healing; physical well-being; counteracting jealousy and envy

INDIGO Psychic visions; meditation; divination; stopping gossip

LAVENDER Aiding peaceful sleep; stopping insomnia; increasing knowledge; heightening intuition; easing anxiety

LIGHT BLUE Peace and harmony; protection; baby boys; moving house

LIGHT YELLOW OR GOLD The masculine; justice in legal matters; prosperity; general healing; a quick turnaround with luck

ORANGE Soothing healing; strength in fighting addictions; fun, laughter, and joy; self-expression and creativity

PINK The feminine; romantic love; improving marital relations; finding your soulmate; healing rifts in relationships; baby girls

PURPLE Spiritual matters; protection; banishing evil spirits; contacting guides and angels; breaking bad habits; anything relating to business or self-employment

RED Improving sexual passion and sexual potency; boosting vitality; strength of the mind and body; resolving conflicts; competitions and sports

SILVER Lunar magick; meditation and visualization; prophetic dreams; better communications with others; stability and security

WHITE Can be used as a substitute for all situations; purity and peace; balance and harmony; protection from bad luck; small children; seeking the truth; making your poppet

Example #1: You might want to help your small child do well in sports day, so you would take white cloth and stitch it with white thread (for small children) or red thread (for competitions).

Example #2: There may be someone around you who is unwell, so you would choose orange fabric (for soothing healing) and light yellow or gold thread (for general healing).

Herbs and Their Magickal Influences

There are literally thousands of herbs with magickal uses, so it is worth browsing the web to find out which ones are suitable for your task. For now, we have listed some popular, influential herbs you might like to try. All of these are easily grown from seed in adequate lighting conditions and can be placed on a windowsill or in the garden. If you don't have a green thumb, you can buy your plants or used dried herbs instead. You might also want to refer to chapter 3, on nature's secrets, to incorporate the appropriate flower, plant, or tree life into your creation, or you might favor the use of herbs—the choice is yours.

ANGELICA (*Angelica archangelica*) For protection for a person or place; attracts positivity and repels negativity; removes hexes and promotes patience

BASIL (*Ocimum basilicum*) For love, romance, and fertility; drives away fears and weaknesses; for money, wealth, and prosperity

BAY LEAF (*Laurus nobilis*) For protection from lightning; used in exorcisms; improves mental clarity and dispels confusion

BERGAMOT (*Citrus bergamia*) For protection from illness; money luck and prosperity; promotes restful sleep; stops outside interferences, such as gossips and difficult people

BORAGE (*Borago officinalis*) Strengthens a person's courage; develops psychic powers; wards off evil

CATNIP (*Nepeta cataria*) For conception and fertility; any poppet involving cats; protection from psychic attacks while sleeping

CHAMOMILE (*Matricaria chamomilla*) Reduces anxiety and stress; ushers in financial good fortune; heals both mental and physical issues

CHERVIL (*Anthriscus cerefolium*) For becoming one with your spiritual self; contact with the divine source

CHIVES (*Allim schoenoprasum*) For protection from self-indulgence; helps focus on weight loss

CINNAMON (*Cinnamomum verum*) Anything to do with sexuality, passion, and love; enhances spirituality and raises spiritual vibrations

COMFREY (*Symphytum*) For safety when you are away from home or traveling; buying and selling houses, real estate; strength and stamina

DILL (*Anethum graveolens*) For use when longing for love; attracts women; for house blessings; seeds are used for money rituals

ECHINACEA (*Echinacea purpurea*) Keeps the body healthy and strong; wards off colds and flu; draws in money and wealth

FENNEL (*Foeniculum vulgare*) For avoiding curses and stopping the evil eye; healing and protection from illness; helps virility

FEVERFEW (*Tanacetum parthenium*) For migraine sufferers; helps headaches; provides protection from danger, accidents, and flu-like illness

GARLIC (*Allium sativum*) For protection from the evil eye or anything negative; purifies spaces or objects; guards against black magick; for willpower and self-control

HEATHER (*Calluna vulgaris*) For appearing more attractive to others and enhancing popularity; for protection against crimes; encourages peace in the home

LAVENDER (*Lavandula*) Promotes peaceful sleep and happy dreams; cures insomnia; helps heal depression

LEMON BALM (*Melissa officinalis*) For healing and success; increases psychic development; aids nervous disorders

LOVAGE (*Levisticum officinale*) For love and eroticism; bring success results in court settings; for prophetic dreams and astral projection

MARJORAM (*Origanum majorana*) Cleanses the soul after a time of stress; eases nightmares; dispels anything negative

MINT (*Mentha*) For enticing spirits and internal purification; raises energy levels; for prosperity in business

MUGWORT (*Artemisia vulgaris*) Helpful for backache sufferers; calms neuroticism; increases the power of any spell; often used alongside other herbs to boost their power

PARSLEY (*Petroselinum crispum*) Increases libido; protects the home from intruders or anything negative; brings about a sense of wellbeing; attracts prosperity and abundance

PEPPERMINT (*Mentha balsamea Wild.*) Clears away sickness and ill health; works well for any kind of eating disorder

ROSEMARY (*Rosmarinus officinalis*) Stimulates the memory; improves learning and exam results; for all-around good health

SAGE (*Salvia officinalis*) Banishes negativity and evil spirits; clears and cleanses homes of negativity; helps a person cope with grief; magickally promotes a long and healthy life

SPEARMINT (*Mentha spicata*) Anything relating to respiratory problems such as asthma; for strength and vigor

THYME (*Thymus vulgaris*) For better organization; attracts faithfulness and fidelity; wards off thieves and keeps material possessions safe

VERBENA (*Verbena*) For love wishes; protects against lightning and storms; keeps a person youthful, both inside and out; brings about nice dreams

Example: If you worry about your partner's fidelity, you would use dark blue fabric sewn with dark blue thread (for fidelity) and stuffed with a small amount of thyme (attracts fidelity).

Personal Items

Because a poppet pertains to an individual, it is wise to add an item belonging to the person to the doll. A lock of hair works well. If you really want to get down and dirty, you can include fingernail or toenail clippings. This is quite an old-fashioned method of poppet-making, but because these items actually sprouted from the person, it really does give more clout to the effigy. If, on the other hand, you want to help a person without their knowing, it might be best to take a few strands of hair from their hairbrush or comb. A tiny piece of fabric from their clothing or a piece of discarded jewelry will also suffice. If all that fails and you don't have anything at all belonging to the person but still need to help them, you can obtain a photograph of them (nowadays with social media, this is easily done). Or you can simply write their name on a small piece of paper and insert it inside the poppet.

You can sew buttons on the face of the doll for eyes or, if using a fabric such as felt, you might like to draw on the facial features using a marker pen. Yarn can be applied to the doll's head to represent hair; just be sure to match the color of the yarn to the person's hair.

Once you have packed the doll with the stuffing, herbs, and personal items, you can stitch the opening closed. It doesn't matter if the poppet looks nothing like the person. The main fact is that while creating it, you have subconsciously projected your thoughts on to the poppet, considering its purpose and how best this effigy will help your target.

There is no right or wrong way to create a poppet, but it is important to use the correct herbs and colors for the matter at hand. By doing this, you will have far more success with the outcome.

Blessing

Like with any magickal object, it is important to bless and cleanse the item before any ritual takes place. You should have already put your own intent into the doll, but you need to prepare it and cleanse it so that it goes on to work in a positive way. Instructions for blessing your doll are included in the Instructions for Creating Your Poppet (see pages 71–72).

Spellcasting

Once you have created your effigy with the correctly colored material and appropriate items inside, you must light one or more candles that match either the color of the chosen material or the thread. A spoken incantation must be said over the doll three times. When you have done this, you need to close the spell by saying, *"So mote it be."* The candle(s) must then burn down on its own. Do not blow the flame out or the spell will not work.

It is also vital that you do not create a poppet to hinder or harm (see below).

HARM NONE

It is vital that you do not create a poppet to hinder or harm. There are good and bad people in every faith, but causing distress or upset to another when using magick will only bounce back threefold on its sender, so be warned.

It is true that we all come up against people in life who cause us grief and aggravation. This might be someone who is intimidating your child at school, a demanding boss, or even a controlling family member. You can still create a poppet to stop them in their tracks, but you must also be very careful not to send them any ill will while you are physically making the doll. If you are dangerously angry with them or overly emotional, it might be better to ask someone else to make the poppet for you. Being highly emotional or enraged with the person will only bring about disastrous consequences.

If there is someone around you who is a real pain in the behind and you want to stop them from affecting your life, you can weave your magick in a gentle way. To do this, try and imagine what it would be like if this person turned their attention away from you. Visualize the peace it would bring to your life, and envisage them only in a positive light. If your boss is bullying you, visualize him being nice and giving you helpful direction on projects. If your mother-in-law is usually vicious or condescending, imagine her full of warmth and happiness, treating you with kindness and respect. If your next-door neighbor is making your life a misery, picture them moving into a beautiful new house with roses around the door and a picket fence. Keep those thoughts pure and free of hate and all will be well!

CREATE AND SPELLCAST YOUR POPPET

With all of this in mind, you're finally ready to create your poppet! Follow the general instructions below for specific measurements, cutting and sewing instructions, blessing incantation, etc. Be sure to look at the provided spells for rituals to find your soulmate, easily sell your home, or invite more cash flow into your life, among others.

Instructions for Creating Your Poppet

When creating a poppet, you can use the following instructions, customizing the colors and ingredients to fit your particular goal. The spells we've provided on pages 73–81 detail color and herb information for you. Remember to create your poppet with good intent in your heart and mind.

Materials

12 × 12-inch (30 × 30-cm) piece of fabric in the appropriate color (see pages 63–64 for a list of colors and their meanings)

Chalk or fabric pen

Fabric scissors

Pins (optional)

A spool of thread in the appropriate color

Synthetic or organic stuffing, such as straw, rice, Poly-fil®, cotton, etc.

Herbs of the appropriate variety (see pages 65–67) for a list of herbs and their meanings)

Personal item from the target

Pen and paper

White tealight candle

A candle in the appropriate color for your task

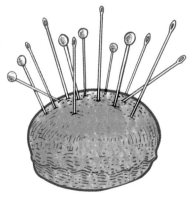

RITUAL

Take the fabric in your chosen color and fold it in half, wrong sides together. (Your poppet can be any size you like, but around 6 inches (16 cm) in length is probably about right.)

Use a piece of chalk or a fabric pen to draw the outline of your doll on the folded fabric. Then, take the scissors and cut out the doll shape. (You may want to pin the edges of the fabric together for easier cutting.) When you're done, you should have two pieces of cloth that mirror each other.

It's time to stitch the poppet together. When choosing your thread color, look at the list of colors once more (see pages 63–64) and use a shade that represents your situation. It could be the same color as your fabric, or it could be another color, to aid in additional ways. Sew your poppet around the edges, leaving an opening for stuffing.

Pack filling material into the poppet. You can use any kind of synthetic or organic filling, but be sure to leave space for herbs, paper, or any other items you might want to place inside the doll to enhance its power.

Once your doll is comfortably stuffed with room to spare, you'll want to add the herbs, personal items, and paper with the name of your target, if using. (If you plan to use a specific spell from pages 73–81, put its recommended herbs and trinkets into the poppet at this time.)

When you are finished, light the white tealight candles and place them on your altar, on either side of the poppet—it's time to bless your poppet before use. Say this blessing three times while the candles burn:

> *"All negative vibes in this doll begone,*
> *With this gentle light, I shall harm none."*

Allow the candles to burn down. Once they have extinguished themselves, your poppet is ready for the next stage.

Recite an incantation appropriate for your use three times (or use the incantation from the spells we've listed). Your poppet is finished and ready to perform its task.

Spells for Relationships

When casting spells for relationships, it is always best to make two dolls. One that represents you, and the other to symbolize the other person.

A Spell for a Happy Relationship

Materials

Fabric color: Pink, for femininity and love, or light yellow/gold, for masculinity

Thread color: Dark blue, for domestic bliss

Herbs: Basil, for love and romance, and cinnamon, for anything to do with sexuality, passion, and love

Candle color: Pink, for love

RITUAL

Make each doll using the instructions for *Creating Your Poppet* on pages 71–72 and the materials listed above. Kiss each doll before lighting the candle(s). Speak this incantation three times:

> *"With fondness and a charming kiss,*
> *We will dwell in undisturbed bliss,*
> *To love with all that is divine,*
> *Yours and mine, our hearts entwine."*

After you've recited the spell three times, close it by adding *"So mote it be."* Place both poppets together in a drawer.

A Spell to Meet Mr. or Ms. Right

Make two poppets: one representing you and one representing your future partner. Begin this ritual on a Friday evening when the moon is full.

Materials

Fabric color: Pink, for femininity and love, or light yellow/gold, for masculinity

Thread color: Orange, for fun, laughter, and joy

Pen and paper

Herbs: Dill, for longing for love, and verbena, for love wishes

Candle color: Pink, for love

Other items: A medium or large gardening pot; gardening soil

RITUAL

Make each doll using the instructions on pages 71–72 and the materials listed above. On the paper, write all the qualities you would like in an ideal partner. Pack this into the doll along with the herbs. When you are finished, light the candle, place it and the poppets on your altar, and recite the following incantation:

*"New love I seek, hear my plight,
This message I send to you
this night, I bring you close,
I draw you near,
Love begins
when you are
here."*

After you've recited the spell three times, close it by adding *"So mote it be."* Place a large-enough pot of soil outside your front door and bury the dolls in the pot. It can take anywhere from a few days to a month for the spell to work.

A Spell to Heal After a Relationship Ends

Make only one doll for this spell.

Materials

> Fabric: Use material from a piece of your old clothing (color is not important)
>
> Thread color: Yellow, for healing
>
> Herbs: Mugwort, to enhance the spell's power, and marjoram, to relieve stress
>
> Candle color: Lavender, to reduce anxiety

RITUAL

Make your doll using the instructions on pages 71–72 and the materials listed above. Recite this incantation three times:

> *"I call all angels to heal my soul,*
> *To be free of emotion, this is my goal,*
> *Send my old love on his / her way,*
> *I live in hope for happier days."*

After you've recited the spell three times, close it by adding *"So mote it be."* Keep your poppet by your bedside for a month. Your pain should lessen as each night passes.

Spells for Money

Every now and again, an unexpected bill drops on the mat and we might not have enough money to pay for it. It could be that each month you struggle to balance the books or have to pay for an appliance that broke down or suddenly need to see the dentist. It is not a crime to ask the spirits for money as long as your need is genuine. Often, if you ask the universe for cash, it will only give what is required, so people wanting to sweep up a jackpot could be sorely disappointed.

A Spell to Attract Extra Cash

Perform this spell on a Wednesday during a new moon phase.

Materials

Fabric color: Green or dark yellow/copper, for money

Thread color: Green or dark yellow/copper

Herbs: Chamomile and echinacea, to attract wealth

Other items: A few coins; a magnet

Candle color: Green, for money

RITUAL

Make the doll using the instructions on pages 71–72 and the materials listed above. Include the coins and/or magnet when stuffing it with the herbs and personal item of your choice. Repeat this incantation three times:

> *"Fill my wallet with a wealth of cash,*
> *This is my need and not for greed."*

After you've recited the spell three times, close it by adding *"So mote it be."*
Keep the poppet in your bag or pocket for the following few weeks.

A Spell to Boost Business

Perform this spell on a Thursday during a waxing moon phase.

Materials

> Fabric color: Purple, for business or self-employment
>
> Thread color: Green, for money
>
> Herbs: Mint, for business, and lemon balm, for success
>
> Candle color: Purple

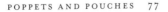

RITUAL

Make the doll using the instructions on pages 71–72 and the
materials listed above. Repeat this incantation three times:

> *"Remove all toil, eliminate stress,*
> *Shine down your power and bring success,*
> *Goddess of wealth, I summon you near,*
> *My business is great, this is my fate."*

After you've recited the spell three times, close it by adding *"So mote it be."*
Keep the poppet somewhere near your cash register or the area where
you do most of your work.

A Spell for Selling or Moving House

Whether you are having difficulty in selling your property or simply want to move to a new home, this poppet will help remove any obstacles.

Material

Fabric color: Brown or light blue, for real estate/moving

Thread color: Brown or light blue

Herbs: Lemon balm, for success

Other items: Citrine crystal, to remove blocks; a small seashell, for movement; a garden spade

Candle color: Brown or light blue

RITUAL

Make the doll using the instructions on pages 71–72 and the materials listed above. Include the citrine crystal and seashell when stuffing it with the herbs and personal item of your choice. Light the candle and repeat this incantation three times:

> *"Change the place that I shall dwell,*
> *With citrine, lemon and a shell,*
> *A move for me, I soon shall see."*

After you've recited the spell three times, close it by adding *"So mote it be."* Allow the candle to burn down until it extinguishes itself. Using the garden spade, bury the poppet outside of your property, in your garden, or in a plant pot. When you do finally move, remember to dig up your poppet or the new tenants may not reside there very long.

Spells for Healing

If you need healing strength while facing a physical or mental problem, poppets can help immensely. Make sure you place personal items inside the poppet, making it very clear who the poppet is for and what the problem is. It is also a good idea to write the sufferer's name and ailment on a piece of paper and place this inside the doll.

A Spell for General Healing

This poppet will cover almost any illness.

Material

> Fabric color: Light yellow or gold, for healing
>
> Thread color: Light yellow or gold
>
> Herbs: Rosemary, bergamot, echinacea, and peppermint, for good health; and/or lavender, mugwort, and parsley, to ease depression and anxiety
>
> Candle color: Light yellow or gold

RITUAL

Make the doll using the instructions on pages 71–72 and the materials listed above. When preparing your paper, write the sufferer's name and the ailment you wish to remove. Repeat this incantation three times:

"Angel and goddess of healing, I pray,
To take this illness and cast it away,
Fill them/me with strength, let good health shine,
With your magickal love sent from the divine."

After you've recited the spell three times, close it by adding *"So mote it be."*

A Spell to Banish Negative People from Your Life

We all encounter people who make life difficult at some stage or another. The poppet you create for this spell will represent the person you wish to banish. Make the front half of the poppet white and the back side black. This symbolizes you banishing the dark and bringing in the light. Remember to perform this spell with good intent.

Materials

Fabric color: 1 piece in white, for good, and 1 piece in black, for bad

Thread color: White, for purity

Herbs: Garlic, fennel, and sage, to remove negativity

Other items: Garden spade

Candle color: White, for neutral feelings

RITUAL

Make each doll using the instructions on pages 71–72 and the materials listed above. Make the front of the poppet white and the back black.

With the candle lit on your altar, repeat this incantation three times:

"I banish you from time and space,
No more shall I see your face,
I cast you out with a rightful mind,
All traces of you, I leave behind."

After you've recited the spell three times, close it by adding *"So mote it be."*

Allow the candle to burn down until it has extinguished itself. Take the poppet to a field or wooded area (somewhere in nature) and bury it under a pile of leaves or soil. The person in question will disappear from your life, though no harm should come to them.

Magickal Pouches

Magickal pouches are made in a very similar way to poppets. They are also a form of keepsake that contains the power projected into them, just like a poppet. You can either create a drawstring pouch yourself by using materials and threads in appropriate colors, or you can buy one from a store. Inside the pouch, you place little items and herbs that represent the issue you wish to solve (just like with a poppet). Then the pouch is placed on the altar next to an appropriately colored candle. An incantation is spoken over the pouch to amplify its power. Pouches filled with love and joy make wonderful gifts, especially for weddings, christenings or Wiccanings, birthdays, or Yuletide— sending luck and success to the receiver. You can read more about pouches in-depth in our book *Wiccapedia*.

Chapter 5

Pentacle Power

THE PENTAGRAM, ONE OF THE EARLIEST RECORDED symbols used in many cultures across the world, is a five-pointed star. The meaning of each of the five points of the star differs slightly from one culture to another, but they are widely understood as characterizations of the elements: earth, air, fire, water, and spirit.

The number five is significant and implies all things human. We have five fingers, five toes, five basic senses—smell, taste, sight, hearing, and touch—Christ was said to have five wounds on the cross, and, in Islamic faith, there are five daily prayer times. We can even juxtapose the image of a human standing with arms and legs outstretched onto the star.

Neo-pagans used the pentagram in ceremonial magick and rituals, drawing the five-pointed star in the air with a wand or athame. This is nice to do before commencing with any kind of ritual, as it is thought to offer protection to the witch while they weave their magick.

PENTACLE COLOR MAGICK

For the purposes of spellcraft and Wiccan magick, there are six different-colored pentacles. Each pentacle represents certain life issues and has a specific color known to positively influence the challenge at hand. Within this chapter we cover the six corresponding topics:

1. Family and friendships (BLUE)

2. Money and wealth (GREEN)

3. Health and well-being (YELLOW)

4. Love, marriage, and relationships (PINK)

5. Work and business (RED)

6. Spiritual matters (PURPLE)

For each color and topic we list a description of benefits, an example dilemma, and an incantation, all meant to illustrate how you can ask the pentagram for help. Choose the colored pentacle that represents a situation you might need some help with.

Focus on the pentacle for a few minutes and then activate its energy by reciting the provided incantation (or an incantation that feels appropriate to you) out loud. Speaking your desire directly from your heart will help you connect with the pentacle's power and will give more meaning to your request. These are lovely exercises to do every day, just using your pentagram and a lit candle.

· BLUE ·

Family AND Friendships

**A BLUE pentacle can benefit any situation
involving children, friends, or relatives.**

EXAMPLE: You have warring children and wish for
them to get along better. Hold your left hand over the top
of the blue pentagram above and say something like . . .

*"I summon the power of the pentacle today to heal
the rifts between* [children's names].

*Let them be kind to one another
and be friends rather than enemies.*

So mote it be."

· GREEN ·

Money AND Wealth

GREEN is the color of the pentacle benefiting this area of life.
Tap into the universal pot by politely asking for a little more.
If you ask the universe for cash, it will likely only
give what is absolutely necessary.

EXAMPLE: You've been hit with an unexpected bill and are not sure where
you'll find the money to pay it. Holding your left hand over the green pentacle,
speak openly, and tell the pentacle exactly what the money is for . . .

*"I call upon the universe for an increase in my cash flow.
I have received an unexpected bill, and I have no way of paying for it
without your assistance. Please send a little extra wealth to me this day.*

So mote it be."

· YELLOW ·

Health AND Well-being

**All matters affecting health can be drawn
upon with the healing color, YELLOW.**

EXAMPLE: You are not sleeping properly and find yourself
tossing and turning most nights. Hold your left hand over the
yellow pentagram and describe what relief you need . . .

*"I ask the angels of slumber and relaxation to
allow me a peaceful sleep this night.*

*Once I am far away in dream sleep, don't let me
awake until I am completely refreshed.*

So mote it be."

· PINK ·
Love, Marriage, AND Relationships

**Whether you are single or in a relationship,
any issues relating to your love life or passion
can be helped with the color PINK.**

EXAMPLE: You have been single for a while and feel ready to seek a
new life partner. Hold your left hand over the pink pentacle
with warmth in your heart and recite . . .

*"I ask the angels/goddesses of love to point me
in the right direction so that I might find my true love.
Allow me to be part of a couple and to share my life
with someone special. Bring new love my way.*

So mote it be."

· RED ·

Work AND Business

**If you are having difficulties at work or simply
want to boost your business potential,
pull on the power of the RED pentacle to assist you.**

EXAMPLE: You are hunting for a new job and need help in finding
exactly the right one. Hold your left hand over the red pentacle,
envision your success, and say . . .

*"I ask the universe this day to shine a path
ahead of me and guide me in the right
direction so that I might find a new job.
Bring luck and good fortune to my working life.*

So mote it be."

· PURPLE ·
Spiritual Matters

You might want to feel closer to someone who has passed on, unlock your psychic talents, or ask the spirit world for help with your meditations. Use this PURPLE pentacle to connect.

EXAMPLE: You seek to become more psychic and raise your vibration. Hold your left hand over the purple pentacle and, with your goal in mind, repeat . . .

"I open my mind and body to the power of this magickal symbol
and ask that you give me the insight to
become more spiritual and intuitive as each day passes.
Please help me to tap into my second sight.

So mote it be."

PENTACLES VS. PENTAGRAMS

A basic five-pointed star is known as a *pentagram*. However, when it is inside a circle, it is referred to as a *pentacle*. The surrounding circle represents protection to all humanity and the five elements within. For witches today, the pentacle is a sacred symbol that appears on many altar items. Often spells are cast on top of flat pentacle-engraved objects, and candles are positioned on the five points of the star to give more potency to spells. Many believe that the star holds its own special power, an energy we can frequently draw upon to help us in our daily lives.

When the pentagram is turned upside down, it assumes a goat-like shape that in some neo-pagan faiths symbolizes the horned god. At some point in Western history—likely in the twentieth century—the five-pointed star became erroneously equated with Satan and devil worship. As time went on, those working on the darker side of magick adopted the down-turned pentagram sign. Because of this, and likely because most witches want to practice purely healing or natural magick and not associate with negative symbolism, we typically use the pentacle in the upright position.

Part Two

SPIRITUAL
MAGICK

Chapter 6

Meet Your
Spirit Guides

MANY PARENTS REPORT THAT THEIR CHILDREN HAVE
imaginary friends, and psychologists believe that they are a natural
part of a child's healthy development. For most, it is a way of a child
taking control of their lives and feelings and, more importantly, helps
with their creativity and self-esteem.

Read on to learn about author Leanna's experience with her childhood imaginary friend, which grew alongside her to become something else entirely.

LEANNA'S PERSPECTIVE

From my earliest memory, I had an imaginary
friend called Erik. I didn't set a place for him at the
table or blame him for the small mishaps around
the house. I never even saw him in his physical form. He visited
me each night, just before I went to sleep, and his image would appear
behind my closed eyes. He was blond with piercing blue eyes, and each
time he arrived, I felt like I was being hugged, with huge, loving arms
around me.

Erik was always the same age as me, and unlike most children whose
imaginary friends disappear over time, mine didn't leave. He stayed with
me throughout my childhood and on to adolescence.

I was three when Erik showed me my first vision. These revelations
would always happen as I was drifting off to sleep. A few years later when
I was eight, one night I saw a mental picture of my best friend at school
falling from her bike and scraping all the skin off the right side of her
face. Erik spoke to me and said not to get upset and that she would be
all right, so I drifted into sleep, thinking nothing more of it. The next
morning, I relayed the message to my mother over breakfast, describing
in detail what I had seen and how my friend had blood all over her face.
My mother was very good to me and never disputed what I said. A few
days later, as Mother and I were waiting at the preschool gates, my friend
arrived, and just as Erik had shown me, all the skin was scraped from
the right side of her face. I stared at her, at which point her mum, who
obviously thought I was distressed, said, "Don't worry Leanna, it looks
worse than it is. She just took a tumble when she was riding her bike!"

As I grew older, so did Erik, and I would often dream of this young, fair-haired man, talking to me or giving me counsel whenever I was dealing with certain issues in life. It was only as I reached my teenage years that I realized he wasn't an imaginary friend at all—he was my spirit guide!

What Are Spirit Guides?

Spirit guides are souls, like us, that have reincarnated multiple times and over many thousands of years. During their incarnations, they will have dealt with almost every situation you can imagine and experienced all the human emotions that give us the knowledge and wisdom we need to evolve spiritually.

When a soul reincarnates repeatedly, it reaches a certain level of perfection, and although most guides are by no means perfect, there does come a point in the reincarnation process when they do not have to visit the earth plane anymore. This is because they simply can't learn anything new; instead, they are allocated individuals on Earth to guide and follow through their lives.

I have read many books that describe guides as being androgynous, but in my experiences, they have always had a gender. I have spoken about Erik, but in my twenties, I was also visited by a female in dream sleep, who I called Jane, mainly because she looks very similar to the actress Jane Seymour. She began appearing when I started having gynecological problems, so it seems that we may have guides who are specialized in certain fields.

About seven years ago, I found out I had another guide called Peter. This happened purely by chance. I am very lucky to have a stepfather who is a qualified, clinical hypnotherapist, and I had asked him for a past-life regression so that I could explore my previous lives. Some weeks later, he put me into a deep hypnosis and I traveled back to a time shortly before my birth in this life. The feeling I had of being in the womb was strangely familiar to me and something I find hard to put into words. I experienced a slight ethereal sensation, like I was cocooned. Then he told me to travel back a little bit further, to a time before I was conceived. As this happened, I was numb and felt totally detached from my body. I made my way through a dark tunnel, and up ahead were the brightest of lights. It didn't hurt my eyes to look—pure love was waiting for me in that light, and I knew I had to get to it as quickly as possible. When I finally arrived, the dark tunnel disappeared behind me until I was illuminated.

Standing in front of me were around twenty people. Some of the faces I remembered, and others I didn't recognize. My parents, my husband, and even my stepfather, who was sitting right next to me, were present in the group. Some of my dearest friends who I cherish in this life were assembled together, and everything was light and white and beautifully hazy. I felt quite emotional for a moment. It was a bit like going to a family reunion where everyone has their focus on you. We were all on the same vibration. Each of us was a little different from one another, but at the same time, I knew that we were all part of one another.

With each minute that I was under the hypnosis and quietly reflecting on the group, I came to understand that, without being told, you know absolutely everything when you die. You will instinctively know the answers to all of the questions you had as an earthly being. The people in front of me were members of my soul family, and as I studied my mother's face, I knew that we had reincarnated together many times before. I had a slight recollection that I had in fact been *her* mother in previous lives and that she had been my sister, cousin, and best friend in others. We had all reincarnated at some point with one another, swapping and changing roles. It was a very bizarre realization. I went on to recall snippets of each life as I quietly observed the group.

Then a figure stepped forward from the crowd and a man I have never met before in my earthly life was standing in front of me. I became very emotional and started to cry. I knew who he was: his name was Peter, and it felt like forever since I had seen him. How could I have forgotten him? Peter smiled and took my hands. It was incredibly strange, because my human brain knew that I had never met him before in my life, but my spiritual self recognized every single feature, from the color and shape of his eyes to the contour of his nose. I had an overwhelming love for him. It wasn't a romantic kind of love; it was much deeper than that. A more intense, safe, and secure love. He telepathically told me that he was my primary guide, and although he had always been there for me, he had taken over for Erik and Jane when I reached maturity.

In the years to come, I continued with my hypnotic regressions and traveled back to my "time between lives" on many occasions. I developed a thirst for knowledge. I needed to keep being reminded of what I already knew so that it could help me understand all the spiritual aspects of life and pass on the wisdom I have been allowed to enjoy.

I feel genuinely privileged to have a connection with my guide and even more fortunate to have been able to visit the spirit world during my hypnoses. I received so much information about the afterlife while I was there—too much to write down in a single chapter—but it has taught me so much, and for that, I am truly grateful.

What I Found Out About Reincarnation

During each hypnosis, I was instructed by my stepfather not to forget any of the information I had received during my visit between lives. Here are just some of the many findings I learned and remember.

Why do we reincarnate, and what's the point?

The entire point of reincarnation is so the soul can evolve. The more lives we have, the more we learn, and with that knowledge, our vibrational energy gradually raises.

We don't always return to Earth. There are many planets upon which we can be born. Earth is one of the more difficult places, where the lessons are harsher, but we can achieve so much more in a shorter time span when we choose to come here.

That word—*choose*—is key is my next recollection. We have a choice as to whether we reincarnate or not; no one forces us to be born. We sometimes feel the importance of reincarnation because we want to remain within our soul family. If our soulmates choose to return to Earth and we don't, then their soul will advance more quickly and they could potentially leave us behind.

Before we return, we are shown a selection of earthly bodies and we must choose one. There are millions of angels and guides in the spirit world, but there is also a higher vibration of beings, often referred to as *elders*. They discuss and help us decide which body we want to reincarnate into and what kind of trials we would like to undergo. This process can take time, but they encourage us throughout to experience lots of life situations so that we can go on to improve our imperfections and gain empathy from our involvement. For example, if someone is weak in character and always controlled by others, the soul would continue to reincarnate into these kinds of people until they learn to be more assertive. We are told the dates of our birth and death in advance. We are also informed of the other soul group members who will reincarnate with us. This explains why, during life, we have feelings of déjà vu or just instinctively know when something is going to happen. It also gives a greater meaning to the idea of love at first sight. We have in fact met our loved ones before and have probably reincarnated hundreds of times with them; so when we encounter them for the first time in this life, we have already loved them and feel like we've known them for years. On Earth, the people we form friendships with are souls from the same family group, and it's often the case that we can be related, married, or lovers in one incarnation but simply neighbors, friends, or work colleagues in another. Our roles might change, but we are still part of the same soul group.

What happens to the soul when we are born?

The soul does not enter our earthly body at the moment of conception. It flits in and out of the fetus throughout the duration of our mother's pregnancy. It takes an entire nine months for our soul to attach to, adjust to, and accept the human body. At the moment of birth, we enter our earthly form briefly, but during sleep and over the next two years, the soul continues to flutter back and forth, to and from the spirit world. It is during this time that we have the choice to either continue our journey on Earth or remain in the spirit world.

As little children, our guides are never far away, and because the soul has recently come from the spirit world, they often have the ability to see and interact with their guides. As the years pass by, they become less visible and speak to us through our dreams and subconscious mind.

Why don't we remember our previous lives?

Before we are born, any memories of the afterlife and previous lives are erased. This is because we must learn each lesson firsthand. If we are able to remember a previous life, it could have an impact on the way we deal with the present situation.

Why do we have to go through so many problems in life?

With each challenge we accomplish, the soul grows and matures. You may know subconsciously that it is wrong to hurt or bully other people. This is because, in a previous life, you have either been the persecutor or have been on the receiving end of a tormentor. You cannot show true empathy until you have actually been through that situation yourself. On the other hand, you may find that you have a deep sympathy for starving children in foreign areas, and that is because you have already experienced starvation in a previous existence. Reincarnation erases the details of each lesson you have gone through, but the soul still holds on to that knowledge. In order for your spiritual self to reach perfection, you have to understand all emotions and see an experience from both sides.

Why do we reincarnate with horrible people?

We might reincarnate with neglectful or abusive parents or have a sibling who we can't abide. On occasion, we might find ourselves in the wrong place at the wrong time and face-to-face with a predator.

These people who we find so intolerable are not from the same soul-group family. There are many varying levels of souls and zillions of soul groups. Before we are born, we often agree to reincarnate with souls from different or lower-level soul groups, to help them grow and evolve and bring them along faster. The lesson not only helps them elevate more speedily but also allows us to raise our vibration by dealing with problematic people or abusive individuals.

Why are we reincarnated with mental or physical health issues?

When a person who has a mental or physical health issue in life passes over to the spirit world, they are completely cured. Often, souls decide to experience a life with a disability. This helps the soul mature quicker and also serves as a learning opportunity for the parents of the child, along with the teachers, doctors, caretakers, or anyone else who helps them go about life more easily. We will all at some point or another experience a life with disability, and we will all be the able-bodied person who is part of a disabled loved one's care and nurturing. When you reincarnate into a body that suffers physical or mental impairments, you climb the spiritual ladder much quicker.

Why are some people wealthy when others live in poverty?

Throughout our reincarnations, we will all at some time experience vast riches and suffer times of financial hardship. When we are born into a rich life, we are watched carefully to see how we manage the wealth. It's a bit like a test. Those well-heeled celebrities who support charities and give a lot away will score brownie points when they cross over. Having very little money forces one's true personality to come to the forefront; it helps us understand the importance of every material object and gives us opportunities to perform acts of selflessness.

Which religion is right?

Every single person who walks the earth has a spirit helper to guide them on their journey, no matter what faith they follow. Our soul is preprogrammed to know that there is a higher power, and religion is just man's way of making sense of it. The guides and elders understand how important it is for humans to follow a spiritual path; they welcome the fact that religion often helps a person strive to be kinder, thoughtful, and more helpful toward others. In truth, most people who frequent churches, temples, and mosques are decent, moral individuals. Guides and angels also love it when we try to connect to our deities. Rituals, prayers, and meditations are vital in enabling the soul to progress. Upon death, everyone is immediately aware of the higher power, and if not, they are educated in the truth of it all. Because we have died, our souls are immediately reminded of the grand design, so we accept everything around us.

When you die, you will discover that there is no set religion. It is just a world in which you can be at peace with exactly who you are.

How do our guides get messages to us?

When we have a niggling feeling about something—call it a hunch if you like—this is a sign that our guides are at work. They communicate with us through our emotions, so if you wake up one morning and have a sinking feeling about something, you must decipher it as a spiritual warning. We don't realize this, but our guides speak directly to us, at night when we sleep and throughout the day. Rather than us physically seeing or hearing them, they plant a seed in our minds that we interpret as our own thoughts or feelings. It's vital that we trust our instincts, because often it is our spirit friends making us feel a certain way.

The spirit world also sends us signs when certain things need to be done or when we need to take a particular direction in life. They can open the doors of opportunity, so if you get offered a job out of the blue, it is likely that your guide is presenting you with a new direction to take. I learned that it is vital to pay attention to everything going on around me in life and to always look at the bigger picture, for there is often a reason why things happen.

When our guides or loved ones in spirit want us to know they are nearby, they can sometimes send things called *apports*. These are small, solid objects, such as tiny crystals, pins, or keys, that manifest from a nonphysical place. Items can be literally anything, but they usually have some significance to the receiver. Another item commonly sent from the spirit world is a single white feather. These represent angelic influence and often appear to a person when they need comfort. Feathers are also a sign of protection, so if you see a white feather in your path, you should know the angels are watching over you and that you are completely protected by the spirit world.

What happens when we die?

During one of my regressions, I went through the death process and was taken to the spirit world. Once I had traveled through the tunnel, I wasn't immediately transported to my final destination like I'd imagined I would be. I found that upon death, the soul first goes to a place comparable to a hospital, where spirit doctors work to cleanse and heal the soul before it can move on. Although there is said to be no such thing as time in the spirit world, this process can take a while, depending on how a person died. If it was a sudden death, the soul can be in a state of shock and will need time to acclimate to their new surroundings. If a person has been very sick prior to death, they will need to have their soul balanced. Higher beings spend time with every person, aligning and purifying their soul, and it is only when this phase has been completed that you can move along to the next part of your journey.

Your guide usually assists you through the next transition, which is entering the spirit world. I was astonished at the true beauty of the spirit world; it was nothing like I could have ever imagined. Although it wasn't dissimilar to Earth, its splendor was enhanced a thousand times. Every detail of this euphoric place is heightened, each droplet of water is amplified, and the flowers sing in unison with the grass. I perceived colors that I have never seen before. I cannot even explain them to you. The mountains are soft pink and lavender in color, and there are even islands in the sky. However, I eventually came to know that everyone's resting place is different. Because the spirit world knows every detail about you, your spiritual place is exactly in tune with your soul and will be exactly right for you. If you were a keen gardener in life, you might end up in the most beautiful garden with all your favorite plants and flowers. If you were a homebody, your spiritual place might be luxurious house catered to fit your exact needs.

Just before a person is scheduled to pass over from the place of transition to the spiritual world, their loved ones, already in spirit, get very excited. Imagine not seeing someone you love for a very long time.

The anticipation of being with them again sends a happy, frenzied feeling throughout the soul group. When you do finally reach them, you have a lot of catching up to do. If for some reason they weren't present at the welcome party, all you need to do is to mentally visualize the person you want to see, and within an instant they are right there with you.

Are we judged when we die?

Every situation we are faced with in life is watched and monitored from the spirit world. How we react to certain situations, the level of kindness we show in everyday life, and how we control our behavior is all paramount to our spiritual development.

Therefore, it is so important that while we are on this planet, we strive to be the best we can be. Each one of us has the ability to make a difference in this world and in the lives of others. No one person is greater than the other. We are all just as important as the next.

On my first journey, Peter took me to a large colonial-style building, where I was met by a group of beings dressed all in white. It was clear to me that they were there to assess the life I had just lived. It wasn't judgment day—far from it. It was simply a time when you are shown all the important events of your life so that you can understand where you achieved or failed in your mission. This can be an emotional time for the soul, but no one reprimands you if you didn't do something right; you are just made to see where you can improve next time. All this information is shown to you with a deep sense of love and understanding from these higher beings. You are also able to delve into the Akashic records (a compendium of all human events, thoughts, words, emotions, etc.) so you can be made aware of your past lives and compare your strengths or failings from then until now.

Only after this evaluation are you free to spend time in the spirit world with those you love. At least, until it is time to reincarnate again.

Is there such a thing as hell?

I have spoken about how your resting place is a reflection of your soul, so the more highly evolved you are, the more beautiful your place will be. Someone who is cruel or unkind or who has committed evil acts on the earth plane might find themselves in a darker place, one far less picturesque than the places given to those who apply themselves to doing good all through life. This place is not hell, but it's not pleasant, either. Whatever place you finally arrive at, you will be assisted by spirit helpers. These guides are proficient in encouraging young souls to reincarnate swiftly so that they can work their way out of this afterlife and strive toward something better.

The Three Key Stages of Spiritual Development

These are the three main categories, but I know there are hundreds of subcategories in between.

NOVICE SOUL or young souls haven't reincarnated very much over the course of time. They can be selfish, narcissistic, aggressive, and abusive and can show cruelty, spite, or jealousy. Often, they do not show sympathy or compassion and can be cruel to animals or people.

INTERMEDIATE SOULS have reincarnated many times and reached a certain level of spiritual understanding. They have an interest in religion or faith. (It doesn't matter what religion the beliefs fall into.)

They are generally kind, caring, compassionate, and hardworking, have high morals, and show generosity. They have a long way to go as far as improving their spiritual status but are on the right track.

ADVANCED SOULS have nearly fulfilled their reincarnation process on the earth plane. They have lived thousands of lives and have experienced nearly every human emotion possible. It is doubtful that you will meet many of these souls in life, as they are few and far between. They have a godly presence about them, are completely selfless, and have great understanding. They value the lives of others more than they value their own and will probably not have to return to the earth plane very much because they are already advancing rapidly. Once an advanced soul has completed their spiritual learning by way of reincarnation, they go on to be guides or will return as "Earth angels" to help a number of people with life problems.

Connecting with Your Spirit Guide

While under hypnosis, any doubt I had about the existence of a spirit world went straight from my mind. Every detail about the afterlife became clear to me. Having met Peter and, more importantly, being able to remember my time with him under hypnosis, I felt that I must learn to connect with him from my earthly bed.

Your guide will never want to frighten you, so it is unlikely that they will suddenly appear before your eyes in the cold light of day. To reach a successful connection, you must be prepared to experience a deeper level of consciousness. It can take a lot of practice to perfect, and only when you are at an advanced state in the meditative process can you begin to see visions. These will usually occur when you are in the middling stage between sleep and wakefulness or in the moments before you wake up. You might also want to keep a notepad and pen next to your bed, as it is common to be told relevant information in dream sleep.

Over the years and with a lot of practice, I have mastered the art of connection. For me, it's like looking at a screen, a bit like a video recording. The background is black and the images appear with gold edges. The pictures move like they would in a video and last anywhere between one and three minutes. Prior to the visions, I sometimes hear a ringing sound, a bit like tinnitus but not as annoying. This is when I know my soul is tuning into a higher frequency and I have finally connected.

Read on for simple tips and steps to help you achieve a connection with your spirit guide.

Items to have nearby

Crystals are very good to dot around the house, as they balance the
energies in a room and can also help you to ground yourself. The seven
crystals below are good if you want to promote successful meditation.
I recommend that you house these stones somewhere in the bedroom.
There is no need to spend a fortune on them when purchasing. Small,
polished versions, or tumble stones, can work just as well as large,
more-expensive pieces. The choice is yours.

ANGELITE Used for summoning guides and angels

AMETHYST A calming stone used to enhance psychic ability and meditation

CLEAR QUARTZ Amplifies healing energy; known as the master healing stone

ROSE QUARTZ Good for relieving stress and tension; restores the aura by
replacing negative energy with positive energy, boosts a love vibration

BLACK TOURMALINE A grounding stone that connects the Earth with
the human spirit; aligns the chakras

AVENTURINE Energizes the Heart Chakra for wellbeing
and calm emotions

CARNELIAN Improves concentration
during meditation

Mindful meditation

I began with a series of meditation
techniques when first trying to connect
to Peter. Before embarking on any spirit
communication, it is imperative that
you mediate for at least thirty minutes.

Lots of people find it hard to meditate for thirty minutes, but once you get the hang of it, it's very easy. Those of you who have researched meditation will know there are hundreds of ways to get into a meditative state. There is also a wealth of information online that can help you find the right method for you.

If you choose to perform your meditation during the waking hours, select a crystal and hold it in your hand. If you want to use all of them in your meditation, sit and space the stones in a circle around the base of the chair you're using or on the floor, should you choose to go without a chair. If you hope to meditate during your sleeping hours, situate the stone(s) either under the bed or next to wherever you are sleeping.

Make sure the house is quiet and sit or lie in a comfortable position. You don't have to be in the lotus position (sitting with legs crossed and hands on knees) as depicted in some books; just make sure that you are cozy, snug, and completely relaxed. I find lying in the fetal position, under the covers, in my bed the best position for me. You might prefer to lie on your back or sit upright. It's completely up to you!

First, concentrate on every part of your body, starting with your feet. Relax the feet, focusing on each toe being completely floppy, then work up the body to the ankle, calf muscles, and so forth. Your aim is to be totally still, allowing yourself to become calm and tranquil. When you get to the area below the waist, hold a pelvic floor exercise for ten seconds, then clench your buttocks for a few seconds and relax. When you get to the top part of your body, raise your shoulders up toward your neck for five seconds before releasing them. You will feel a tingling sensation as they fall back to their usual position. Take your time. By the time you reach your facial muscles, you should be feeling extremely relaxed.

Second, breathe steadily, either through your nose or mouth—whichever is most comfortable. Take a deep, slow breath inward and then exhale slowly. Repeat this for a few minutes or until you start to feel weightless. Clear your mind. Behind your closed eyes, focus on the darkness you see. See if you can pick out any shapes or lights.

Ask questions

At this stage, you should be in a meditative state, so now is the time to ask your guides for information. In your mind, ask your guide a series of questions, focusing on each question for a few minutes.

> "I would like my guide to visit me. Are you there?
> Can you show yourself to me?"

You might see patterns and shapes behind your eyes or feel a strange sensation of belonging. The experience is different for everyone. If you don't feel anything, don't be disheartened. Remember, some guides will not show themselves to you while you are awake and might wait until a time when you are asleep. They know you better than you know yourself and may think that you are not ready to receive them in a conscious state.

> "Please show me your gender.
> Are you male, female, or nonbinary?"

At this point, you must tune in psychically and trust your inner thoughts and instincts. Imagine you are standing in front of a being. Tap into the energies and trust your very first answer.

"Can you tell me your name, please?"

It might take several meditations before you receive this answer, but, once again, trust those instincts—you have them for a reason. Allow your imagination to expand. Your guide's name may not come quickly or even come to you at all when meditating. You might be given the name a few days later, so look out for signs. If, during the following days, you hear the same name repeatedly, perhaps on TV or the radio, it could be your guide nudging you gently. Alternatively, you might wake up one morning with a clear name in your head.

Once you have your guide's name, you are on your way to connecting with them fully.

If you are serious about making a connection with your guide, you must meditate every night before going to sleep. People often fall asleep during meditation; this is quite all right. When you arrive at a meditative state, your vibration rises and your energy starts to change and evolve. It does take lots of practice, so never give up. After a while you will be able to slip into this relaxed state quickly and summon your guide as needed.

Automatic Writing

Automatic writing, or *psychography*, as it is also known, is a way of psychically channeling your spirit guide to connect with you. This is a very good exercise to do straight after a meditation, because you need to be in a trance like state for it to work.

Pen and Paper

For me, the best way to get a positive result is to use pen and paper, although if you can type faster than you can write, you might find the computer to be a better option.

Sit at a table with your paper in front of you. Light a white candle to clear any negative energies in the room.

If you are a beginner, it might be worth setting a fifteen-minute timer; short bursts of writing often give better results. Close your eyes or wear a blindfold. Ask your spirit helper to come through you and guide your hand.

Start writing on the paper. It doesn't matter what you are writing. You can start with your name and how you are feeling or you can just randomly write letters of the alphabet in some joined-up words. I usually start by writing my guide a letter, something like this: *Dear Peter, please can you enter my subconscious today and guide my pen, sending me a message from the spirit world?* (Don't be surprised if your writing resembles that of a six-year-old, either.)

You can also start by writing down or asking a question out loud. There may be something you want to know, such as whether you will get a new job soon, whether your children okay, if your health is going to improve . . .

Good questions you might like to start with are as follows:

"What is your name?"

"Are you my guide?"

"Do I have a guardian angel?"

"Will my worries subside soon?"

"Will I get a new job?"

"Will I find a nice relationship?"

Literally write down anything at all you that desire to know. Write down or speak the question aloud, then concentrate on the pen and begin to write.

You might start to feel your fingers tingling, or you may get a light-headed feeling. This happens when you have reached a connection with your guide.

Do not stop writing at any one time. Do not cross out or erase anything or worry about grammar or spelling. Try to get into the zone and feel the magick come from the pen, and continue to keep your eyes closed.

Decoding spirit messages

After around fifteen minutes of writing, open your eyes and read it back. Some of it might be garbled or make no sense at all. Don't worry too much about that. A word might not be spelled correctly, but you might be able to make out what it reads, or it could be in the form of an anagram:

olve = love, or Mynmaesiwillam = My name is William.

When you become more experienced, you will psychically get into the zone and your messages will become clearer to read. Remember, practice makes perfect, so you should have a go at automatic writing every day. Just make sure the house is quiet, the TV is off, and no one is going to disturb you.

Demons, Devils, and Monsters

So far in this chapter I have covered subjects that rest on the positive side of spirit communication, but it is also important to understand that while tapping into this state of consciousness, we are also targets for darker energies, such as demonic beings.

Witches do not believe in the Devil because the term is a Christian concept, and Wicca practitioners do not believe in Christianity, but this doesn't mean malevolent entities are not out there. When we connect on an astral level, we can occasionally encounter a more disruptive soul who can appear to us as demonic, evil, or sinister. They are drawn to the purity of a more advanced soul, a bit like a moth to a lightbulb, so it is vital that before you begin to tap into the other side, you know how to protect yourself.

Evil spirits thrive on our fear, which makes them stronger, so it is best not to give them a reaction, even if you feel scared or intimidated. These spirits often materialize when you are in the deepest of meditations; you might see an ugly face behind your closed eyes, or worse, attract something into the room with you. If this happens, you must summon the archangel Michael. Also ask your guides to protect you and surround you with a golden light. I have come across these kinds of souls on more than one occasion, and I find the best way to deal with them is to speak to them in terms they understand—basically, I tell them to get lost. I show no fear and in no uncertain terms tell them that they are not welcome and to leave immediately. I have had a 100 percent success rate with this method and every time, they just disappear before my eyes! One of the ways you can stop them entering into your meditation is to perform a short ritual before you begin any kind of meditation.

Prepare with a prayer

Lie in a comfortable position and imagine you are in a beautiful purple or golden bubble. For a few minutes, visualize a white light shining down upon your body. In your mind, say this prayer.

> *"I call upon all of the positive universal forces, my angels, my guides,*
> *and my loved ones in spirit, to protect me during my connection.*
> *Wrap me in your protective love and bring only*
> *the sweetest of souls to my being."*

An incantation for evil encounters

Memorize this chant for immediate use if you have an unwanted visitor. Repeat these words over and over until the evil spirit has gone:

> *"I call upon archangel Michael, healer and protector:*
> *Remove this entity from my face,*
> *Delete this image from my mind,*
> *Banish this evil through time and space,*
> *Bring only those that are pure and kind."*

The Rainbow Bridge

Many people who are spiritually inclined have a love of animals. We cherish our pets, which often become our substitute children, and indulge them in all manner of pampering, so it is no mistake that we regard them as important members of our family. In some ways animals are more significant than humans because they do not have a voice. While communicating with Peter some years ago, he informed me that animals do not have any karma. Their purpose on Earth is to teach the human soul compassion and to help us connect to a higher vibration. By understanding the animal kingdom, and indeed by respecting every creature, from a tiny spider to a huge whale, we elevate and purify our aura. Referring to the previous explanation of a soul's advancement (see pages 108–9), those who do not like animals are probably younger souls that have not reincarnated very many times.

When our animal friends die, the grief we feel can be just as distressing as it is when losing a human member of the family. Some years ago, three of my dogs died within eight weeks of one another and I was distraught, to say the least. I had read about the Rainbow Bridge: a place where animals are thought to go when they die. It's described as a beautiful, warm, outdoor place where our pets reside until it is our time to die. When we pass over, it is thought that our beloved pets become very excited at the prospect of meeting us again and will come greet us. We can spend time with them in the spirit world, reunited with our treasured companions.

Shortly after my beloved dogs passed away, I asked Peter if they had reached the Rainbow Bridge safely and whether he could send me a message or a sign that they had indeed crossed over. Around six o'clock the following morning, I had a vision. I saw my uncle Bob, a devout animal lover who had passed away some years before, in a beautiful field where the sunlight bounced off the grass. He was playing with my lovely Border Collie, Gwen. Her brown coat glistened in the sun, and she was bounding around with endless energy. Suddenly, she swiftly shape-shifted into a stunning apricot standard poodle. At that point my uncle Bob walked over to me and smiled. He said he was a "keeper of animals." He went on to tell me that people who dedicate their time on Earth to animals, often go on to take care of people's pets in the spirit world until their owners join them.

If you're grieving a lost pet and the prospect of waiting until death to rejoin them seems unbearable, rest assured: animals who have passed over do come back to their owners from time to time. Here are the signs that they may have paid a visit:

1. **You dream of your pet.** When we sleep, our vibration is higher, so spirit people and animals find it easier to connect with us.

2. **Before dropping off to sleep,** you might feel like something is sitting on the bed, or you may experience a feeling of something heavy sleeping in your arms or nestled into your back.

3. **You feel something**— your spirit cat or dog—brush up against your leg when you least expect it.

4. **You hear a faint bark,** or the cat flap will open on its own.

I was more than happy to know that my uncle is watching and caring for my lovely dogs while I continue with my life, and I am sure that when I pass over eventually, I will be reunited with them once again.

How to Live Happily Ever After

Always be kind to yourself. You are not perfect, and that is the reason you are here. Everyone has a purpose in life, whether it be to overcome certain obstacles or to serve other people. Never question "Why is this happening to me?" You have chosen this path for a reason, and however problematic or challenging your life is, you have agreed to experience it and will grow from the involvement and knowledge you acquire. Life is hard; it is a huge, global classroom where you come to learn difficult lessons. Look back on some of the toughest times in your life and ask yourself whether you would change what you have learned. If you hadn't undergone those hardships, you wouldn't be able to help or empathize with others who are going through something similar. There are moments of joy in life; you must embrace them and keep them in your memories. But for now, understand that you are a part of the divine source that is seeking perfection, and this quest takes time—sometimes spanning many lifetimes. Never rush yourself or be false. Recognize your faults and practice being a better person. Invite a little spiritualism into your life every day, and give yourself time think and to reflect on why you are here.

Even when your insides are screaming, always try and be kind to others. A difficult child or a meddling mother-in-law might actually be a young soul you agreed to help. Try to be patient with everyone, for we are all going through life at different tempos. Remember, your spirit world might be different from someone else's, so to strive toward the beauty beyond, aim to be the very best that you can be—in this life and those to come.

Chapter 7

Superstitions
and Omens

FOR THOSE OF US WHO HARBOR A SUSPICIOUS NATURE,
watching a mirror smash to the floor or seeing someone deliberately walk
under a ladder sends shivers down the spine. Even straight-laced types
who would never dream of believing in such nonsense might encounter a
spate of bad luck and convince themselves that a black cloud hovers over
them. Where do these beliefs come from? Is there any credence to them?

Omens and superstitions are similar and send us signs that good
or bad luck is coming our way. Although some folks dismiss them as old
wives' tales, there are millions of people who feel there must be some
truth to them.

After all, nearly every civilization the world over has superstitions—they've been around for thousands of years.

Each culture has their own set of omens and superstitions based on population, history, disasters, and the like, and we include a number of them here. Do bear in mind that this is hardly an exhaustive list. It would be easy to deliberate over superstitions and omens day and night for weeks, and at the end we would still have more to learn.

You will no doubt recognize some of these beliefs, while others may be new to you. Even though superstitions are mostly rooted in ancient times, there are plenty that have evolved over the decades and hundreds that we still keep alive today.

THE ORIGINS OF OMENS

Although the word might bring to mind the term ominous, omens originally weren't meant to scare anyone. In ancient civilizations, diviners were tasked with communicating with the gods. They interpreted certain occurrences as signs, determining whether they contained messages of either inherent good or evil. So, for example, if a shooting star burned brightly in the night sky, it was up to the diviners to say whether this was a prediction of something good (like a bountiful crop) or bad (a natural disaster on the horizon).

Even now, there are people who look for blessings or curses in events like eclipses, hurricanes, and epidemics. When these occur, you can bet your life that a group will come out of the woodwork to say the event is punishment or reward for some human action. In 1997, for instance, the Heaven's Gate religious cult located in San Diego, California, took the appearance of the Hale-Bopp comet as an omen. The cult leaders preached that committing suicide would allow them to hop aboard a spacecraft hidden within the comet's tail and escape Earth. They saw its arrival as a reward and believed that only they could recognize and act upon it. Sadly, many men and women died by following this belief. This example highlights how seriously omens can sometimes be taken.

SEARCHING FOR SIGNS

Even though some people may believe that believing in omens is a relic of the past, plenty of us still live our lives looking for "signs." This makes the practice of sighting omens very much alive today. Think about some of the article headlines you see: "10 Signs You're Headed for Success" or "15 Signs Your Relationship is on the Right Track." If you read postings like these, you will find plenty of room for interpretation; signs are never hard and fast but may indicate what lies in your future. Articles like these are not the kind of cryptograms likely to live on in folklore, but there are other, time-tested omens that most of us recognize and many of us believe may predict the future.

SUPERSTITIONS AND OMENS

The main difference between omens and superstitions is that superstitions usually require some kind of action (or avoidance), while omens just appear or happen. Some of the most popular superstitions have origins in religion—in fact, some people believe religion is just a form of superstition—where others sprung up in ancient civilizations. Whatever the case, there is usually a communal belief around the consequences of an act that keeps people wary or encourages them to take part. Either way, the superstition is usually meant to prevent something from happening, rather than encourage the person to find a new solution.

For example, a football fan might wear the same sweatshirt every Sunday, believing he has to do so in order to prevent his team from losing. Maybe this started because this person was wearing this particular sweatshirt on the day his team won a tough game and the team's been on fire ever since—when he wears this sweatshirt. Note that the fan takes personal responsibility for the win or loss instead of saying, "Well, you can't win them all" and accepting that loss is going to happen at some point. Either way, he is definitely not willing to chance a loss caused by his not wearing that shirt.

Whether we realize it or not, many of us recognize omens and participate in superstitions on a regular basis. Here are some that are fairly common:

Birds, Animals, and Insects

ANTS If you see a line of ants in your path, never step over them, as this will bring you bad luck.

BEETLES The deathwatch beetle, a wood-boring insect, is probably the most feared in superstition. If it creeps over your shoe or you hear it in the walls, a death will follow. Some believe that if you safely carry the beetle outside, you can counteract its curse.

BIRDS However unpleasant, any bird pooping on your head is thought to be good luck.

BLACK CATS Different cultures see black cats as either good or bad luck. In the west, they were believed to be witches' familiars so were considered bad luck if they crossed your path. Today, both witches and nonpractitioners alike adore black cats and are trying to break the stigma of these often persecuted creatures.

BLUEBIRDS These birds are a reminder that happiness is coming, even if you don't feel it right now.

BUTTERFLIES If a butterfly enters your house, important company will arrive soon to give you good news.

COWS To hear a cow moo after midnight means evil is nearby.

CROWS There are so many superstitions surrounding these birds, but the most common is what it means to see them in groups. One crow signifies bad luck. Two symbolize good luck. A group of three represent good health. A group of four are signaling that good wealth comes your way. Five crows represent approaching ill health. And six deliver news of death.

DOGS If a dog is walking between two people, the couple will soon break up. If one follows you home, it is a sign of luck and good things to come. If a random dog enters your home, you will meet a new friend soon.

DRAGONFLIES Seeing a dragonfly signifies change, maturity, deeper wisdom, and peace.

GOATS In Rwandan societies, eating goat meat is thought to make women grow beards.

HARE It is rare to see this magickal lunar animal, but if you do, you will be showered with good fortune.

HORSESHOES These were hung as talismans on the outside of doors to protect the home from goblins, who were thought to fear metal. Nowadays if the horseshoe points upright, it signifies good luck to the residence and acts as a house blessing. If the horseshoe points downward, all the luck will run away.

LADYBUGS A passing ladybug, or ladybird beetle, is a sign that happiness is coming to you. This is especially true if the bug lands on you.

MAGPIES Seeing magpies in multiples means different things, according to the nursery rhyme "One for Sorrow." One magpie is a symbol of sorrow or bad luck. A pair represents joy. Three magpies means a pregnant mother can expect her child to be a girl, and four means she can expect a boy. Five magpies represent silver, and six gold. Seven are "for a secret, never to be told."

OWLS These creatures have been present in folklore for centuries. Place an owl's feather inside a baby's crib and it will keep evil spirits away. In the northern regions of England, people are very superstitious about owls and won't even have an image of the bird in the home for fear of bringing bad luck.

PEACOCKS It is unlucky to keep the feathers of a peacock in your house. This could possibly be because of the eye shape present on the feather, which resembles the evil eye.

RABBITS A rabbit's foot is often worn or carried as a protective accessory. Saying "white rabbits" three times on the first day of the month will bring luck throughout the coming weeks. While a rabbit's foot can be worn for protection from bad luck and negative spirits, rabbit amulets made of precious stone, metals, coins, or jewels are also an option—and are less harmful to rabbits. Sometimes an amulet will have a protective prayer or incantation carved into it.

RAVENS In the United Kingdom, the tame ravens that reside at the Tower of London hold lots of superstition. It is thought that if the birds leave, the crown of England will be lost.

RED CARDINALS This little bird signifies that you need to take care of yourself, or it may remind you to be clearer with your thoughts and intentions. It may also step in your path when a deceased loved one is present and keeping an eye on you.

ROBINS If seen in the garden, these delightful little birds are a joy, but if one enters the house, news of a death will follow.

SPARROWS To see a pair of sparrows together means that new love is on its way. If a sparrow enters the house, a death is predicted.

Some Other Superstitions

APPLES Peel the fruit in one long strip and toss it behind you, over your shoulder. Does it land in the shape of a letter? This is the initial of the name of the person you will marry.

BABIES Laying a baby on its left side was once thought to cause left-handedness, which was frowned upon many years ago. Babies born with a caul—when the amniotic sac surrounds the infant's head and/or body upon delivery—are indeed rare, and the caul is believed to mark the baby with good luck for life. Exposure to moonlight was also believed to cause cleft lips. Because of this, mothers-to-be took great care to stay indoors while gestating.

BIRTHS There is a nursery rhyme titled "Monday's Child" that states, "Monday's child is fair of face/ Tuesday's child is full of grace/ Wednesday's child is full of woe/ Thursday's child has far to go/ Friday's child is loving and giving/ Saturday's child works hard for a living/ But a child born on the Sabbath day/ Is blithe and bonny, good and gay." In other words, the child born on Sunday is the best of the bunch!

BREATH Holding your breath while passing a cemetery is thought to prevent evil spirits from entering the body through the mouth.

CANDLES A candle blowing out by itself mid-flow or with no explanation predicts a death in the near future. Blowing candles out on a birthday cake and making a wish is said to grant your desire. A pink candle burned on Valentine's day will bring love to you. A candle that will not light means a storm is coming. Lighting candles at births, deaths, and marriages prevents evil spirits from coming near the participants or family members.

CHIMNEY SWEEPS It's thought to be good luck if you touch or kiss a chimney sweep, particularly on New Year's Day. (Author Leanna has a log-burning stove and will not let the chimney sweep leave until she has planted a kiss on his or her cheek.)

CLOTHES/OBJECTS As with the football-fan example, many people have "lucky" items or accessories that they wear for tests, interviews, trips, sporting events, or special occasions. Accidentally wearing clothes inside-out is believed to bring about good luck. Kids can wear pajamas inside-out when they are hoping for a snow day.

DREAMING Dreaming of death signals good luck is coming. Dreaming of a wedding indicates a death will soon occur. Dreaming of a white candle means true love is coming.

FOUR-LEAF CLOVERS A rarity believed to be a sure sign of luck. If you find one, pick it, press it in a book, and keep it forever. In Ireland, all clovers are believed to be good luck, whether they have three or four leaves.

FUNERALS Counting the number of vehicles in a funeral procession will bring about a death in the counter's family.

GRAVEYARD DIRT If you have dirt on your shoe from a cemetery, you should put it under the steps of your home for good luck.

HANDS If the left palm itches, you will receive some money. If the right palm itches, you will have to pay some out. To stop the itching, place your palm on some wood.

HEADACHES Pain about the right eye indicates a mother or sister will visit. Pain over the left eye means that a brother or father is coming.

ITCHING or ringing in the ears means someone is talking about you.

KEYS If you drop your keys, place them on wood immediately for good luck.

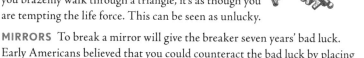

LADDERS When a ladder is set up, it forms a triangle with the surface it's leaning against. Triangles represent life in some traditions, so when you brazenly walk through a triangle, it's as though you are tempting the life force. This can be seen as unlucky.

MIRRORS To break a mirror will give the breaker seven years' bad luck. Early Americans believed that you could counteract the bad luck by placing the broken pieces of mirror in south-flowing water for a period of seven hours. One other theory is to bury the broken mirror in ground awash in moonlight. In Jewish tradition, because mirrors were thought to be portals to all other realms, they would be covered following a person's death. If you failed to cover them, the spirit of the deceased might be trapped on the earth plane, unable to move on. If a new couple accidentally catches sight of themselves in a mirror, then they will have a long and blissful marriage.

MOON It is thought that the full moon stops you from sleeping. Trust us, this is true!

NIGHTMARES Some believe bad dreams are premonitions of bad luck, even if the unlucky event is not visualized in the dream.

PAVEMENTS Step on a line and you'll break your spine, or step on a crack and you'll break your mother's back. This probably originates from the fact that uneven pavements might be dangerous to walk on.

PENNIES If you find a penny on the ground facing heads-up, it indicates good luck. Pick it up and keep it! Heads-down is the reverse and is a sign of bad luck. Best to walk away and leave it for someone else to find.

PREGNANCY Seeing a pregnant woman at a funeral is believed to be bad luck for the baby. Hanging a gold ring on a piece of string over an expectant mother's stomach is thought to foretell the sex of the child. If it moves in a circle, the baby is female. If it moves left and right, it's male.

RAINBOW These natural phenomena are believed to be signs of good things to come or blessings.

SALT If you spill salt, you must toss some over your left shoulder to avoid bad luck. In da Vinci's painting of the last supper, you can see that the salt is spilled in front of Judas, Christ's betrayer. People saw this and started to associate spilled salt with bad luck. It was also believed the devil is behind each person on their left-hand side, so tossing a little salt back that way would blind him and keep him away.

SEVEN This number signifies good luck. Many people play the number seven when gambling. It has roots in biblical symbolism and ancient cultures.

SHIPS Women on ships were once thought to bring about bad luck, but probably only because they were a distraction for sailors! But a nude woman was welcome aboard (oh dear . . . of course) because she supposedly calmed the waters. Therefore many ships have a nude female figurine on the bow.

SHOES In British culture, putting shoes on a table predicts a death in the family. This comes from England, where a deceased miner's shoes would be placed on a table as a sign of respect.

SHOOTING STARS Wishing on one is supposed to ensure you get what you want.

SILVERWARE Dropping silverware indicates that company is coming, with a dropped spoon signaling a child, a dropped fork indicating a woman, and a knife representing a male. Dropping a tablespoon means an entire family will be visiting. A knife falling and sticking into the floor indicates that bad luck is on the way. If you drop two spoons and they land in a crossed position, then either someone will be getting married soon or someone is having twins.

SNEEZING People used to congratulate one another on sneezing, as it was thought that evil spirits were leaving the body. It changed over to "God bless you" for much the same reason and as a hope that the evil spirits would stay out. Also, some societies believed that a hard sneeze could release your soul, so a "bless you" would help keep it where it belonged!

STARS Wishing on the first star of the night means you will receive your heart's desire.

THIRTEEN This number is believed to portend bad luck. Friday the thirteenth, for instance, is thought to be an unlucky or even a dangerous day. Some traditions believe this is because the Last Supper had thirteen guests (Judas being the thirteenth), and because Christ was crucified on a Friday.

THREES The synchronicity of three is common in daily life. If there are two deaths in a community, for instance, it's believed a third will closely follow. It also refers to general bad luck, such as three failed tests, three flat tires, etc. The third person to light a cigarette off one match is said to be cursed. However, threes can also work in positive ways, by good things happening in threes.

TIME 11:11 These numbers, or any repeating numbers, are thought to be good luck and a sign of wishes granted. This has become more common with the use of digital clocks.

TRAVELING Especially on a Friday, traveling is bad luck. This also relates to starting a vacation on a Friday: the entire trip could be ruined!

UMBRELLA People used umbrellas as parasols, to protect themselves from the sun. Opening an umbrella indoors is believed to anger the sun god and bring about bad luck.

WEDDINGS So many superstitions befall the simple wedding.

Bridesmaids In years gone by, a bride would choose a selection of close friends to protect her from evil spirits.

Cake In ancient pagan times, there would be two cakes: the groom's cake and the wedding cake. Both were made from fruit to symbolize fertility. Grooms sometimes still have cakes in modern weddings. Placing wedding cake under your pillow is thought to cause dreams of the one you will marry.

Catching the Bouquet It is believed that when the bride throws the bouquet backward, whoever catches it is next to be married.

Confetti Years ago, guests would throw grain or rice at the bride and groom to ensure fertility and prosperity. This tradition has continued into modern times, with some variations.

Days of the Week This folk rhyme dates back to a time when weddings could take place on any day with very little planning. "Mondays for health, Tuesdays for wealth, Wednesdays are best of all, Thursdays for losses, Fridays for crosses, Saturdays, no joy at all!" This practice has changed for practical reasons (since most people work during the week). Now the majority of weddings are on weekends.

Dress It is thought to be unlucky for the groom to see the bride in her wedding dress before the ceremony.

Rain This sign is more good luck than bad, as rain on a wedding day is thought to foretell fertility, cleansing of the past, unity with the groom, and the final tears the bride will shed in her marriage.

Ring The ring is a symbol of eternal love.

Something Old, New, Borrowed, Blue Traditionally for luck, the bride should wear something old, something new, something borrowed, and something blue. Another Victorian tradition was for the bride to have a lucky silver sixpence in her shoe.

WISHBONES The person who gets the bigger side in a tug-of-war will have their wish granted.

WHISTLING The act of whistling in the house is believed to attract evil spirits or unfortunate events—particularly the house burning down.

WOOD Knock on wood to prevent bad luck. Most people start this superstition off by saying something positive—"My car has been running great," for instance—and then, so as not to jinx their good fortune, will knock twice on wood.

YAWNING Today, we cover our mouths while yawning out of politeness. Back in ancient times, we did this to prevent evil spirits from flying into the body!

Well, how did you do on these little lists? Did you find that you believe in more omens than you thought, or have you known all along that these things guide you? Will any of these cause you to be more observant or careful?

If you're starting to see a lot of symbols indicating good luck or bad luck, it might help for you to meditate on a specific intention. With this firmly in mind, keep observing what types of omens pop up!

Good or Bad

Generally speaking, actions or beliefs that give people comfort are good—as long as they are not limiting that person's life or harming someone else in the process. If you have a friend who believes in omens or superstitions you find questionable, ask yourself if this belief is bringing the person comfort. If so, then what harm is in it?

There's no doubt that that you've heard and possibly followed other superstitions throughout your life (maybe without even realizing it). Ask your older relatives if they know of any superstitions from their upbringing. Some of them may be popular; others may be more personal, starting when something good or bad happened—kind of like the football fan with his sweatshirt. We tend to want to capitalize on anything that brings us good fortune and eliminate anything that causes bad events, so forming these habits makes sense.

As you start to develop your psychic senses, you may come up with rules of your own; others may refer to these as superstitions. For example, we talk often throughout this book about cleansing your space or setting up a crystal field for protection. If you find rituals like this helpful, then you might not just want to continue; you may also want to share them with friends who have the same interests! Write these beliefs down and take note of how they evolve and change for you—after all, superstitions change with the times, perhaps because we grow more knowledgeable. Of course, sometimes there is no explanation for why things do or do not happen. You can call it luck, you can call it energy, you can call it whatever you want. This is why we keep superstitions around!

Chapter 8

Angelic Numerology

ANGELS HAVE A UNIQUE FORM OF COMMUNICATION for when they want to speak to us. Pythagoras said some variation of the credo, "Numbers rule the universe," and angels believe this to be true. So what is angelic numerology? Angelic numerology is quite simply a sequence of numbers you might see in your mind or dreams, or that, like an earworm with a song, might keep repeating over and over in your head. Celestial angels use a different form of language to gain your attention and deliver a message. In this chapter, we list angelic numbers and their associated meanings, which will give you the opportunity to connect directly with your higher power for advice.

WHO IS MY ANGEL?

Let's talk about who our angels are. Christian scripture and Jewish literature tells us that angels have special powers and duties, and even have various ranks. Archangel Michael is one of the higher deities, having done battle with a dragon, while Gabriel is the angel who announced Jesus's impending birth. Raphael is the angel in charge of healing the sick. Seraphim are angel-like creatures stationed above God's throne, said to have six wings— although they only use two for flying. Cherubim, meanwhile, sit around the throne and praise God constantly.

Though angels are present in many religions, the term *guardian angel* is never used in the Bible. There are clues that imply, however, that these protectors are nearby, including, "For He shall give His angels charge over thee, to keep thee in all thy ways" (Psalm 91:11). So we know that beings watch over us, guide us, and can intervene in dangerous situations.

As we saw in chapter 6, many people believe that we all have a guardian angel assigned to us at birth, and this angel is with us throughout our entire lives.

Angels are not simply human spirits who have passed on to a nonphysical plane; they are immortal entities tasked with looking out for the welfare of all creatures on Earth. Wiccans believe guardian angels can provide you with guidance and wisdom when it's needed most. All you have to do is ask.

Here is an important distinction: although you may have a loved one in spirit who is nearby and might communicate with you, your angel plays a different role. Where your deceased grandmother may not be able to communicate with you telepathically, your angel can. Your angel can give you wisdom and guidance beyond your years and experience. We'll talk more about angel forms of communication toward the end of this chapter, but for now, just think about the differences between a mortal human and an ethereal, otherworldly creature, as well as what those differences mean in terms of the information they can offer.

Although angels have their roots in Christianity, nowadays many believers from every faith trust that they have an angel, or even numerous angels, guiding them. You don't have to be religious to have a helpful angel by your side; you can still be Wiccan or pagan and use angels in your spell craft. You merely need to believe in the many realms that we all inhabit and that the angelic beings are blessed with abilities that we can't even imagine! An open mind is key to learning.

NUMBERS GAME

This is an easy way to make a direct connection with your angels and speak with them every day. You will need strips of paper in pieces just big enough to write a number on. You will also need a container to hold them in, such as a large jar, vase, or bowl. You may want to choose a pretty vessel that complements your interior style or work space aesthetic; you may be turning to it for many weeks, months, or years to come.

Cut one hundred little strips of paper. On each one, write the numbers one to one hundred. In the end, each piece of paper should have a number written on it. Place all the labeled paper strips into the container of your choice, whether it be jar, bowl, or shoebox. Keep your copy of *The Witch's Way* close by for reference, with this section earmarked.

Whenever you feel you need guidance from an angel, or when you just want to connect with an otherworldly realm, reach into the bowl or jar and pull out one slip of paper. Before you choose a number, though, take a moment to say hello and ask for guidance. Although this can be a quick process, take the time to truly focus. You can simply close your eyes, bow your head, and say something like, "I ask you, my guardians, to guide me to the message you wish me to receive today. Help me understand whatever I am about to receive. Let me also be open to other messages from you during the day."

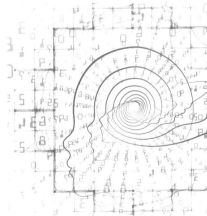

Now that your guardians know you're paying attention, reach in, swirl your hand around, and choose a slip of paper. Then pick up this book, open to the list below and on pages 141–47, and read the message associated with the number you pulled. When you are done, put the numbered slip back in with the others and mix them up again.

Here's what your angels are saying:

1. **Open your heart to someone who is difficult.**
    Take time to understand them and guide them wisely.

2. **Prepare for a change of scenery.**
    A new journey awaits you, so be brave and venture forward.

3. **Let go of an old grudge.** It is not right to harbor resentment.
    If you let it go, you will feel better.

4. **Put your inhibitions to one side and do something spontaneous.**

5. **Ask a loved one for help.** If you are feeling low in spirits,
    share your fears with another.

6. **Write an overdue letter.** Someone from your past misses you;
    you will make their day.

7. **Offer an apology.** Think about your actions in the past
    few months and put right any wrongdoing.

8. **Release your fears.** Conquer your weaknesses
    and you will not have to relive old lessons.

9. **Love is coming your way.** Someone new is to
    enter your life.

10. **Your prayer will be answered and your worries will soon pass.**

11. **Follow your instincts.** Listen to your inner voice, for I am speaking directly to your consciousness.

12. **The impossible is possible.** Take a chance and do something new.

13. **Acknowledge your strengths.**
Your angel is proud of your accomplishments.

14. **A financial windfall is coming.** Don't worry; your finances will improve and all will be okay.

15. **Believe your dreams.** I speak to you in dream sleep, so pay attention.

16. **Your enemies will be silenced.**
Have the strength to stand up to those who wish you ill.

17. **Family is your fortune.**
Cherish your loved ones and wrap them in your heart.

18. **Keep your head held high.** You are stronger than you think.

19. **Ignore the critics and do the best you can.**
You will achieve everything in the end.

20. **Protection is all around you.** You are never given anything you cannot cope with.

21. **Your health will improve.** Eat properly and sleep long and you will begin to feel better.

22. **You will have the patience to overcome adversity.** Trust in yourself.

23. **Kindness is never wasted.** Do a kind deed for someone else today and you will be rewarded.

24. **You are surrounded by love.** Your angels love you so much—remember that.

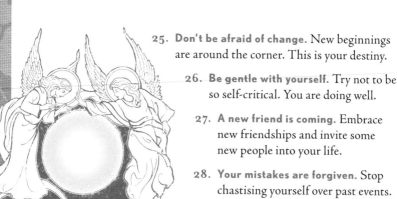

25. **Don't be afraid of change.** New beginnings are around the corner. This is your destiny.

26. **Be gentle with yourself.** Try not to be so self-critical. You are doing well.

27. **A new friend is coming.** Embrace new friendships and invite some new people into your life.

28. **Your mistakes are forgiven.** Stop chastising yourself over past events.

29. **You have worked hard recently and your efforts will be rewarded.**

30. **Honor yourself.**
Take time to meditate and listen to your inner thoughts.

31. **Let go of the past.**
Think only about the future and the good you can do.

32. **An old friend is thinking of you.**
Connect with someone from your past. Now is the time.

33. **Focus on a new dream.**
Don't be frightened of trying new things. You will succeed.

34. **Be an example to others.**
Fill your life with honesty and others will follow.

35. **Offer forgiveness to someone who isn't sorry.**
They may be a younger soul than you.

36. **An unexpected event will occur in the next few days.**
Deal with it wisely.

37. **What you believe to be true, is.** Trust your instincts.

38. **Focus on eating healthfully.**
Food is fuel, so make sure to look after your body.

39. **Prepare for the past to repeat itself.** Old lessons will surface again.

40. **Even if it is just a few coins, donate to charity today.**
Give a little and spread the fortune.

41. **Create harmony in your world.** Sit quietly and listen to peaceful music.

42. **A friend will bring joy to you.** A baby will be born soon.

43. **Tough times will turn around.**
This long road of stress will soon come to an end.

44. **Try a new creative hobby.** It will make your soul sing.

45. **Take the time to listen to a family member.** They need your support.

46. **Count your blessings in life and cherish all your comforts.**

47. **Keep a cool head and try not to be angry with something or someone.**

48. **A child will excel in life through your input and guidance.**

49. **Release yourself from bad habits and start a new regime today.**

50. **Try to release all forms of jealousy; Allow someone the freedom
to follow their chosen path.**

51. **Love conquers all.** Gather the family together for a nice meal
and the opportunity to share your experiences.

52. **Prepare for busy times; the next week is going to be demanding.**

53. **Pay extra attention to animals or pets.**
They need you to care for them.

54. **Share your insight with someone younger.**
They will listen to you and remember your wisdom.

55. **You will change your residence in the future.**
Living in a new home is your destiny.

56. **Ask the angels for what you want and we will help you achieve it.**

57. **Read some spiritual literature today
and try to evolve your soul.**

58. **Learn from your errors.**
Try not to repeat your past mistakes.

59. **Look at those around you.** Remove
yourself from difficult individuals.

60. **Let go of sadness and think only of the
happiness you can have in the future.**

61. **Offer support to someone today.**
A kind action will help your soul develop.

62. **Express yourself to whoever needs to hear it.** Speak only the truth.

63. **Appreciate the beauty around you.** Take a walk in the outdoors.

64. **Embrace positivity.** Tomorrow will be a good day for you if
you are in the right frame of mind.

65. **Ignore the naysayers in your life.**
Move away from those who are negative.

66. **Don't let anxiety scare you.**
Breath in the essence of your angel when you are worried.

67. **Embrace the day and love your life!**

68. **Your loved ones are safe and protected in all that they do.**

69. **Expand your knowledge base.**
Take on a new course or learn something new.

70. **Don't get involved in other people's quarrels.** Keep the middle line.

71. **Colleagues around you could be difficult.** Have patience with them.

72. **Someone you know might be going through a bad time.**
Touch hands with them and try to help.

73. **Speak the truth always, but say it kindly.**

74. **Love your memories, but make room for the future.**

75. **Your guardians watch over you closely.**
We love you and appreciate how hard you try in life.

76. **Believe you will succeed and you will.** Focus your mind.

77. **Rewards are coming to you.**
You have saved up your luck and soon you will see sunshine again.

78. **Listen to someone who needs an ear.**
Offloading their troubles will help them to see the situation clearly.

79. **It is never too late.** Do something you have always wanted to do.

80. **Choose wisely today.**
Be careful when making decisions and listen to your heart.

81. **Do not put off actions until tomorrow!**
Sort out anything that needs doing today.

82. **This world is your school.** Learn all that you can.

83. **Be generous with others.** Give items away that you no longer need.

84. **Treat yourself to something special.**

85. **Clear out your cupboards and create tidiness around you.**
    You will benefit from getting rid of clutter.

86. **Think about someone else today and make a difference in their life.**

87. **Be open to another's opinion.**
    They might not be right, but some truth will be spoken.

88. **Young people might be fractious, so have patience and listen
    to them.**

89. **Let yourself be happy today.** You deserve it.

90. **Relationships need more effort.**
    Spend time together and bring back the love.

91. **A journey by road awaits you.**
    I am guarding and protecting you.

92. **Spend more time sleeping and resting.**
    The future is going to be eventful.

93. **Do what you know to be right, and don't be misguided
    by others.**

94. **Simple joys are best.** Sit outdoors and watch the wildlife.

95. **Visit a neighbor or friend.**
    Your presence will put a smile on someone's face.

96. **Get back into baking and make a delicious treat for those
    around you.**

97. **Spend your money wisely.**
    Do not overspend on things you do not need.

98. **You cannot teach what you haven't learned.**
Others will benefit from your past experiences.

99. **Cut down on unhealthy foods and limit your alcohol.**

100. **Plan a holiday.** You need to unwind and relax.

Combined Messages

Sometimes you may see a number or a sequence of numbers over and over again; many people identify 11:11 to be a significant time of day, for instance. Don't just ignore those instances when you notice them— something from the universe is at play. Combined messages can help make your communication with the angels more specifically.

If you feel that pulling more than one number may be useful for you, or if you would like practice interpreting the message in multiple numbers, then feel free to pull two slips of paper from your jar.

Example: If you choose two papers numbering 76 and 92.

- Number 76 reads:
  Believe you will succeed and you will. Focus your mind.

- Number 92 reads:
  Spend more time sleeping and resting. The future is going to be eventful.

Your angelic message: Your future is going to be eventful, so you need to spend more time resting and sleeping. Focus your mind on self-belief and you will succeed.

Confusing Messages

With any kind of message coming from another plane, there can sometimes be a crossing of ethereal wires—or at least that's how we interpret it. Your angels are never wrong, of course, but they may sometimes be speaking about events that might not happen for some time or about distant event from your past that will relate to a future happening. Remember, time means nothing on the other side; it is just a construct that human beings use to organize events. If you are receiving messages that don't make sense you to right now, write them down. A whole series of events may take place before these messages come to fruition. Have faith. Just wait and see how it pans out.

PREPARING TO RECEIVE

Picking a number from your jar is a nice way to get a quick daily message from your angels. Sometimes, though, you might want more impactful communication, especially when a particular problem has been plaguing you or when your worry runs deeper. In these cases it might help to meditate. This will open your mind to more in-depth information.

Your meditation should focus on clearing the day's worries from your thoughts while simultaneously quieting any distractions. You can prepare your sacred space according to whether you have a specific question (appropriately colored candles, for instance) or whether you need some general guidance.

Many people choose to light a white candle when attempting to connect with their angels, as this color candle represents truth and peace. This will help draw your angel to your side and boost communication. Some also choose to add a rose quartz stone, as this boosts positive energy.

Quartz also helps clear the mind so you can receive and understand the messages coming through.

When your space is prepared and you are in a comfortable position, proceed as you would with any other meditation: Breathe deeply and close your eyes. Allow your mind to open and expand. Focus on your intention. Ask the questions that are on your mind, no matter what they are. And just let the answers come.

If you leave your session feeling as though you haven't received enough insight, know that our angels communicate in some very subtle ways, and not just when we call on them. For example, when you *just know* something is true or untrue, despite all other evidence to the contrary, that is because your angels are telling you it's so. When your intuition kicks in, often it's because your angels are leading you in a certain direction. When you see signs over and over again, guess who's responsible for either putting them in your path or opening your eyes to them? That's right—those busy, busy angels!

In fact, many abilities we consider psychic have some crossover with angel communication. Messages can come through in your dreams—and even your daydreams—so when you wake up with a premonition, you may have picked it up from another source: your angels whispering in your ear while you lay sleeping.

Also, when you are hit with sudden inspiration or an idea seems to come to you fully formed . . . that's a form of angelic communication. It's not to say that you aren't creative or clever; it's just that you have an extraordinary team helping you!

Do's and Dont's

Angels are meant to guide you, not make your life pitfall-free. In other words, even after you connect with them, there will be hard times and trials in your life. But it's during these times especially that you should call on them for help and guidance.

There's nothing necessarily off-limits when talking to your angel. If it's important to you, it's important to them. You can ask for safety (for you or loved ones), clarity, strength, wisdom, or intervention with the divine power on your behalf.

Some people call for guidance every day; others save their queries for major matters. There are folks who swear by calling on their angels when they are gardening, or people who speak to them about their loved ones' activities. Some people make it a practice to speak with their angels before getting out of bed or before they fall asleep at night. Others only communicate with their angels when through numerology. You can do what feels right for you.

However, you might want to make a practice of "checking in" at least weekly, offering gratitude for their guidance and assistance. Remember that your angel is looking out for you and sending you numerology communications, whether you acknowledge it or not. It might be nice to say at least a quick hello and thank-you on a regular basis.

Chapter 9

Your Muse and Cupid

MUSES AND CUPIDS ARE HIGHLY EVOLVED BEINGS THAT come into our lives and support us for one purpose only, staying with us until their task is complete. This happens when it is our destiny to achieve something important, meet someone special, or if we are lacking in incentive to be the best we can.

MUSES AT WORK

In Greek mythology, there are said to be nine muses: goddesses dedicated to philosophy, language, music, and the arts. These inspirational beings, who were themselves graced with many talents, motivated mankind to follow a more creative path. Today, witches see muses as another form of guide, one with an ability to unlock the imagination and set the creative juices flowing. It is highly likely that musical composers and artists, past and present, have or had some kind of connection with a muse. Who knows—when Michelangelo was working on the Sistine Chapel ceiling, perhaps one of these superior beings stood just behind him, inspiring him. It is also very common for writers to express astonishment at some of their written literature. Often they will explain that they have no idea where the words came from or that they just dreamed them up. Where else could their words come from than a muse?

Believe it or not, every single person on the planet is an expert in something. Some may not ever delve deep enough within themselves to discover their gifts, whereas others might fill a lifetime pursuing their burning desire toward a particular interest.

You can call upon a muse whenever you feel the need to explore your creative side. Whether it be painting, photography, writing, or music, a spirit helper is keen to assist you.

In order to be successful in calling your muse, you will first need to make sure that you are in a calm and stress-free environment. A muse is likely to tap into your deep subconscious, so being in a relaxed frame of mind is important if you want to establish a connection with her. More often than not she will visit you at night, just before you drop off to sleep, and transmit an idea directly into your mind. She might also appear in the middle of the day when you are sitting quietly with a blank piece of paper in front of you. Do you feel a sudden urge to write or draw something? That nudge could be a muse whispering into your mind.

An Exercise for Calling Your Muse

If you are dozing or in your bed getting ready to sleep, try to clear your mind of mental clutter and prepare for an imaginary journey. Visualize yourself walking over a field. The image of your surroundings must come from your own subconscious, so with every step that you take, pay attention to the details around you. What is the weather like? Is it sunny and fine, or cloudy and moody? Is there a carpet of flowery meadow grass beneath your feet, or has the ground yet to be ploughed? While you are on this voyage, picture yourself with your arms open wide. Then begin to run. Really feel yourself sprinting, your soul becoming light as a feather the faster you run.

This exercise will help free you of your earthly limitations. It will also help your muse direct her positive energy toward you. Don't worry if you fall asleep during this exercise journey; she will be able to speak directly to your soul, even when you are unconscious, so that when you wake up, you'll be inspired to do something creative.

When you finally rouse from your expedition, make a point of doing something creative. Try painting a picture, turning your hand to a musical instrument writing poetry, or starting that book you've always wanted to write. When you become proficient in the art of connecting with your muse, you won't need the exercise; you will be able to call on her simply by asking for help.

CALLING ALL CUPIDS

Just as we have muses to assist us with our creative talents, cupids are dedicated purely to finding us love. These beings work alongside us regularly, helping improve our emotional attachments. In classical mythology, Cupid is the son of Venus, goddess of love, and Mars, god of war. He is mythologized to fire arrows into the hearts of humans, making them fall in love. Although this is a nice thought, modern Wiccans today believe that there are millions of "Cupid-type" guides out there making sure we pursue the relationships that destiny has chosen for us.

Finding Your Destined Soul Type

Just as there are millions of species of insects and animals on this planet, there are as many different kinds of human beings. Each of us is going through life at our own pace. If you people-watch, it's clear that we are all in categories pertaining to our level of soul development. That is why some of us get along better with one particular sort of person than with others. Have you ever noticed that many doctors and medical specialists behave rather similarly? The same can be said for athletes, or for landlords and landladies, or for caregivers. Each one has certain personality traits and life experiences that pushed them in a certain direction. We believe these like groups are formed from common soul types.

Because humans instinctually yearn to be part of a pair, we often spend our lives seeking out a companion that sits within our soul type. Those couples who think alike (and even look alike, in some cases) tend to be of the same soul group. Some people easily find those their souls feel content alongside; others can end up in relationships with people they have little or nothing in common with. Nowadays people are more selective when choosing a mate, oftentimes waiting until their early thirties or later to tie the knot.

One fact is certain, though: however many partners we may have, each and every one of them is part of our overall destiny. And according to the spiritual beliefs of Wicca, every person you have romantic inclinations toward in this life was chosen for you before you were even born. With that in mind, you might ask, *Why do I have to deal with bad or undesirable partnerships?* The answer is that even those sour relationships are part and parcel of your destiny package, because when we experience a bad encounter with a lover, we will learn and become stronger as a result. We learn something valuable from every relationship in which we are a part. It is thought that throughout our many reincarnations, we agree to pair up with certain souls for a purpose. This purpose could simply be to have children, to experience life with someone undesirable, or even to help another soul evolve more quickly. You cannot teach what you haven't learned, so we face many romantic challenges on our path toward spiritual maturity. Perhaps it's reassuring, however, to think that every single relationship is key to our emerging stronger in the long run.

People desperately unhappy and in long-term marriages clearly need to leave the marriage and move on, but often the cupids will not magickally produce a new match—at least, not until the person has shown the strength and initiative to forge a new path. When courage is shown and a person does decide to distance themselves from an unhappy relationship—oftentimes with the help of family and friends—only then will they be ready to face the next chapter in life. At this point, their soul will have progressed.

Having said that, the cupids do work in mysterious ways and can sometimes intervene. If a person is stuck in a loveless marriage but sees no way out, then perhaps they can weave magick encouraging the cupids to bring them a satisfactory partner. It might well be that it is that person's destiny to have a different partner; simultaneously, it might be the ex's destiny to marry again and have a new family. Sometimes, the person who comes along is a catalyst enabling the marriage to end. Or maybe after meeting the cupids' choice and ending the marriage, this person might spend a year or two on their own so that they can go on to find their own identity. So everything is planned—every little detail. We are all in control of some things in life but ultimately have no control over our fate and our destiny.

Love Magick

If you feel that your love life is at rock bottom or you just can't find the right partner, you can use magick to summon your cupid. They will only assist you if they are allowed, but more often than not they will bring a certain person into your life, whether it be the right or wrong mate for you—with every relationship we experience, we are learning and growing as individuals.

There are certain Wiccan ethics connected to love craft that must be adhered to, and the rule to never influence another person's free will is number one on the list. Magick is incredibly powerful and can change a situation in a matter of days. If you cast a spell for the love of a particular person, the results can be catastrophic to the destiny of that individual.

Let's take a couple examples into consideration.

Example #1: You are head over heels in love with someone who is married, and you've been his mistress for a few years. You decide to use magick to drive him away from his wife. Unbeknownst to you, this action also drives away everything the spirit world had planned for him—his lessons within the marriage and the building of his own personal strength in coming to terms with his relationship, for instance. Another result of your magick is the infliction of pain on his family, such as on his wife and children.

At this point, you are responsible for the karma of all those individuals and are destined to carry that heavy load. Wiccans believe that you get back threefold what you send out, so taking away this man's free will created a ball of negativity around yourself.

So what's the better choice in this situation? If the love you feel is all-consuming and you've reached a point where your life is stuck in the mud waiting for him to make up his mind, then it would be more ethical to cast a spell, not to drive him away, but to help him make a decision as to where his future lies. If he does choose to leave his family, he will make that choice with a clear head. If he is still in a quandary, then, unfortunately, it is time you bow out and leave him to get on with his life.

Let's consider a supposedly less-complicated scenario.

Example #2: You have the hots for a woman a work who hasn't looked twice at you. You grab a battered old spell book and cast a spell for her to fall in love. A week later, she is besotted with you. It could be that your cupid's arrow was never meant to hit her in the first place, though, because she was in fact destined to be with Paula from the accounting department. Now you've blocked that from happening.

She'll spend the next five years hankering after you, and at the end of those five years you'll decide that she wasn't really the girl for you after all. She won't have gone on to settle down with Paula and have the four children they were meant to have—all because you meddled.

The rules and ethics of love craft are indeed complicated, so here is a basic guideline, setting out what is acceptable and what is not:

Dos

1. You can cast a spell for new love, no names mentioned.

2. You can cast a spell for communication with a named person.

3. You can cast a spell for a first date with a named person.

4. If you think someone is keen on you but lacks the courage to ask you out, you can cast a spell for them to find the confidence to ask.

5. You can cast a spell to find your soulmate.

6. You can use magick to help a person make a decision about you.

7. You can cast a spell to make a partner more romantic.

8. You can weave your magick to increase your partner's passion.

Dont's

1. Never cast a spell to win the heart of a named person.

2. Never cast a love spell if you are unsure as to how the other person feels about you.

3. Never cast a love spell for someone who is married or attached to another person.

4. Never cast a spell to split up a couple, even if their relationship already seems doomed.

5. Never cast a spell to cause discord in a relationship.

6. Never cast a spell if you are having an affair with someone who is attached and you want their partner to find out about it.

7. Never weave your magick to entice a named person into an affair.

8. Never cast a spell for love on behalf of another person.

Some Safe and Secure Love Spells

When casting any spells relating to love, it is important that you begin the ritual on a Friday during a full moon phase. Traditionally this is the time when the moon's energy is perfect for love magick, so you will have far more success spellcasting at this time of the month than at any other. Pink is the universal color for love, so any accessories you might want to include on your altar, such as candles and ribbons, should be pink. Red is the magickal color for passion, so if your spell is for strengthening relationships or bringing about more sexual pleasure, make sure your accessories are red. You can set up a small work space or an altar and decorate it with anything that might invoke love to you. Heart-shaped items, photographs, trinkets, or images of cherubs all work well to create the right environment for your spell.

A Spell to Bring Love into Your Life

Materials

A pink candle (to represent love)

Pen and paper

A small white piece of cloth or a handkerchief

A small heart cut from a piece of cardstock

A pair of scissors

A pink ribbon, for love

Your favorite perfume

RITUAL

Place all of the items on your altar, situating your candle in the center. Light it. Write your name on the piece of paper and then, using as many words as you like, describe the kind of partner you want. You might prefer a blond lover with blue eyes, or someone who enjoys sports, the theater, or dining out. This is your wish list, so be as creative as you like.

When you have finished your list, place it in the middle of your handkerchief, folding the paper if necessary, and then place the cut-out heart on top.

Say this spell seven times:

"I desire for my blessings to thrive,
With this spell, romance is alive,
With no earthly binds, my heart is free,
I summon my cupid to bring love to me."

When you have finished reciting the spell seven times, close it by adding, *"So mote it be."*

Snip a small lock of your hair with the scissors and position it inside your handkerchief. Bring all four corners of the cloth together and secure it with the pink ribbon. Lastly, give the pouch a squirt of the perfume, then leave it beside the lit candle until the candle burns out. Once the flame extinguishes itself, move the pouch into your pocket or purse. Carry it for a few weeks.

A Spell to Communicate with the One You Desire

Materials

> A pink candle
>
> 1 teaspoon of caraway seeds (for communication)
>
> 1 teaspoon of dried oregano (for communication)
>
> A small dish
>
> A small aquamarine crystal (for ease with communication)
>
> A small drawstring pouch

RITUAL

In the early evening before it gets dark, light your candle. Mix the caraway seeds and oregano together in the dish. Place your aquamarine stone on top of the herbs. Set the dish on your altar, in front of the candle, and close your eyes. Think about the person with whom you want to communicate. Imagine him or her speaking freely to you and then envisage the two of you being open and honest with each other.

Say this spell seven times:

> *"Open your mind and receive my attention,*
> *No more fear or apprehension.*
> *Open your mouth and speak your words,*
> *Talk to me so you can be heard."*

When you have finished reciting the spell seven times, end the ritual by saying, *"So mote it be."*

Allow the candle to burn down, then pour the oregano and caraway into the pouch. Place the aquamarine stone inside before you close it. Carry this with you when you know you will be in the company of the individual.

A Spell to Summon Your Soulmate

Often we are not allowed to reincarnate with our soulmate, because we would end up being completely absorbed in each other, so much so that we might fail to learn anything while visiting Earth. However, older souls are sometimes allowed to spend their reincarnated lives with their soulmate. If we're not yet allowed to be with our true soulmate, then we can discover partners who are similar to our soulmate. This spell will help you find your right person.

Materials

A chalk board and piece of chalk

A pink candle

RITUAL

On a Friday during a full moon, place your chalk board on your altar and light the pink candle next to it. Write down these words on your board as follows . . .

"Set this spell free, bring my soulmate to me.
With fire in my heart, let our journey start.
Receive this message, walk my way,
Come to me without delay.
So mote it be."

Draw a pentagram at the bottom of the board. Leave the board next to the candle until it burns down. Once the candle extinguishes itself, hang the board somewhere in your house for three days and nights. After that time has passed, erase the words.

On the next Friday of a full moon, (approximately four weeks later) shout out the same spell at the top of your voice. Shouting spells transmit an immense amount of power, so the louder you can yell, the better.

A Spell to Help Someone Decide if You are Right for Them

Materials

Gentle instrumental music

A small lepidolite stone

RITUAL

Go to a quiet room in your house and play some gentle instrumental music on a high volume. Sit in a comfortable chair and cup the lepidolite stone in the palm of your hands.

Close your eyes and envisage the person who needs to make the decision. Transmit your thoughts into the stone and silently will the person to decide whether you are the right one for them. Try not to influence the stone by hoping that you are the chosen one. Think only about the free will of the other person and helping them focus on finally making a decision. Stay with the stone in this frame of mind for as long as you can.

When finished, give your stone to the person. Don't tell them what it is for; just give it as a gift. A short time later, tell this person it's time they made a decision and that you require an answer by the end of the week.

A Spell to Make a Marriage or Relationship Stronger

Materials

A sharp knife

A tall, tapered pink candle in a holder

A small bowl of dried pink rose petals

Yours and your spouse's wedding rings

A 12-inch (30-cm) length of white string or chord

A large pot and some soil for planting

A young pink rose bush

RITUAL

In the morning, with a sharp knife, inscribe yours and your spouse's name into the wax of the candle before placing it in the holder. Light the candle. Place the bowl of dried pink rose petals next to the candle and lay your rings on the top of the petals.

Say this spell twelve times:

> *"These symbols of love shall always entwine,*
> *Our hearts and souls forever divine."*

When you have recited the spell twelve times, close the ritual by saying, *"So mote it be."* Let the candle burn halfway down and then blow it out. Bind the candle with the chord, and when it is cooled, place it on top of the rose petals for the rest of the day.

The following morning, bury the remaining candle and petals in a pot of soil and leave outside. Later, when the season allows, plant a young pink rose bush in your garden. Make sure you mix the pot of rose-petal soil with fresh soil, and rebury your candle in the ground with your plant. As the bush blossoms, so will your relationship.

A Spell to Increase the Romance and Passion in Your Relationship

Materials

A red item of clothing

A photograph of you and your partner

A red candle

RITUAL

When you cast this spell, it is important to wear or hold something red. Place the photograph on your altar and light the red candle. When the candle has burned for about an hour, drizzle a few drops of the wax onto the photo and say this incantation once:

"I call upon the cupids to arouse the passion in our hearts,
Romance is alive and we will strive, to be the happiest we can be.
When our bodies unite in the night,
may we join our souls in splendid love,
With all that is good we ask for your love.
Shower us with magick from above.
So mote it be."

Chapter 10

Spiritual Astrology

THE STARS ARE ONE OF MANY INFLUENCES GUIDING the spiritual realm, and the astrological plane holds multiple varying beliefs and traditions. For example, there are slight differences between Eastern and Western astrology, yet both of these practices are not dissimilar to Celtic astrological beliefs. In this chapter, we will discuss Western astrological signs and how to make the most of them.

It is one thing to know that you are an Aries or a Capricorn and to understand some of the personality traits that go along with your sign. It's another to embrace the spiritual flow of your birth month and allow yourself to reach a higher state of consciousness.

Every birth sign has both good and bad points. Think of the lesser aspects of your sign as opportunities for developing your spiritual gifts. A person born under the sign of Pisces may appear to be dreamy or, at times, out of touch. Instead of just accepting this trait, they could learn to utilize this quality; perhaps a good start would be to meditate upon ways to serve others, help those in need, create inspiring art, or simply engage in prayer.

You may already have a certain amount of astrological knowledge, but whatever your level, there is always a wealth of information left to learn. Spiritual masters can teach you the ins and outs of traversing the starry-eyed walk. To this end, we will blend in words of wisdom from leaders across all disciplines, along with the basic information you need to fully understand the zodiac. We have also included "moonlight meditations" for each birth sign. These can be used to quiet the mind and connect with your sacred self. Practicing these meditations will help you connect with your inner subconscious and sense who you truly are. For a more successful meditation, please note that these are best done on the following moon phases.

- Full Moon When the moon is at its most powerful
- Waxing Moon The three days leading up to the full moon, which is a time to focus on bringing things to fruition
- Waning Moon The three days following the full moon, which is a time to concentrate on removing undesirable things from your life

Spiritual astrology is a vast subject, so those who would like to delve deeper should know there is a huge amount of information online, including educational courses.

ARIES

March 20–April 20

FIRE SIGN

RULING PLANET: **MARS**
SYMBOLIC COLOR: **RED**
GEMSTONE: **RUBY**
PLANT: **TIGER LILY**

"Humility is not thinking less of yourself, but
thinking of yourself less." —C. S. LEWIS

Positive Traits

The ram characterizes **ARIES**, and for good reason. This sign tends
to be focused, obsessive about goals, and confident in their abilities.
They are the "pioneers of the zodiac" and show great ambition.
Whatever they are gunning for they will undoubtedly accomplish.
Aries are high achievers who are usually career-driven. They are also
creative individuals and are always ready for action.

Negative Traits

The ram has horns on its head for a reason: it is a stubborn creature and won't give up without a fight. Aries can come across as obstinate, overly aggressive, cocky, impatient, and condescending. Sometimes they have a short fuse and jump to anger quickly, but on the positive side, they also forgive easily. In the business world, these strong characteristics can be positive and even necessary for survival and growth, but when it comes to personal relationships, these qualities can frequently trip an Aries up.

Relationships

Although Aries are strong-willed and stubborn, they are also respectful and caring. Generosity shines through, and an Aries will always work hard to protect their loved ones. They will fight for love but also need a partner who is less aggressive and able to calm them down.

Moonlight Meditation

Because Aries have natural leadership qualities with a tendency to overdo it at times, there are plenty of opportunities for deep reflection.

On a waning moon, before sleep, speak this incantation repeatedly:

"Under the light of this waning moon,
I give gratitude for the strengths bestowed upon me.
I seek guidance to shed judgment
and impatience, that I might lead by example
and remember my humble nature."

TAURUS

April 21–May 20

EARImagery SIGN

RULING PLANET: **VENUS**
SYMBOLIC COLOR: **BLUE, PASTEL SHADES**
GENSTONE: **TOPAZ**
PLANT: **MALLOW**

> "It is the rain that grows flowers,
> not the thunder." —RUMI

Positive Traits

TAUREANS have an excellent attitude toward work. They are generally dedicated, kind human beings who always try their best in life. They have a lovely sense of humor and possess a positive approach in most of what they do. Being wonderful listeners, they are found in careers as caregivers, counselors, and mentors. Taurus tends to be the stable person in a partnership, looking ahead to the future and how best to get there. Many of these folks have patience in spades and will do just about anything to make things run smoothly. They are creative, artistic, and have lots of friends.

Negative Traits

Taureans are represented by the bull and can be described as tenacious; however, they are also well known for having a mile-wide stubborn streak, which can lead to them locking horns with others. Taureans tend to be opinionated and might tell you in a loud-and-clear (though loving) way that they're right and you're not. Bossy mannerisms and a need to have their say can sometimes make them unpopular, but as the Taurean matures, they are more likely to control their dominance and keep their opinions to themselves. They lean on the side of laziness and don't like mundane chores. This sign is also inclined to be overweight or suffer from weight-related health problems. They love food, and therefore gluttony is often a problem.

Relationships

Taureans have a "stick-to-it" nature and can stay in toxic relationships longer than they should. Eventually, when they reach their breaking point, they usually just switch off and quietly walk away. They make loyal and trusting partners and always put the needs of their spouse first. Learning to see and understand another's point of view is one area Taurus might need to work on. They are sexy, passionate, and need intimacy in their relationship to feel loved.

Moonlight Meditation

Taurus can ask for the wisdom to be more flexible and less obstinate.

On a waxing moon, before sleep, speak this incantation repeatedly:

> *"I give gratitude for the gift of persistence and patience.*
> *I seek the ability to be more accommodating*
> *of other points of view and to value their ideas*
> *as I would my own."*

GEMINI

May 21–June 20

AIR SIGN

RULING PLANET: **MERCURY**
SYMBOLIC COLOR: **BRIGHT ORANGE**
GENSTONE: **TOURMALINE**
PLANT: **ORCHID**

"If light is in your heart,
you will find your way home." —RUMI

Positive Traits

When **GEMINI** are happy, they are the life of the party and the center
of attention. This sign has a genuinely loving and caring nature
and feels emotions deeply, both positive and negative. Gemini
are always up for a new adventure and love to talk to people from
different backgrounds and experiences. They can balance the
anxiety of decision-making by using meditation, deep-breathing, or
aromatherapy. Being smart, they have no problem adjusting to life's
problems. They have a sense of fun, a childish charisma, and a carefree
approach to most challenges.

Negative Traits

Gemini's symbol is the twins, which represent Gemini's natural indecision perfectly. What Gemini wants on Monday, he or she does not want by Tuesday. By Wednesday, that decision may have taken off in an entirely new direction. They are a little contrary, to say the least!

When their mood dips, it can go extremely low, bordering on depressive. Being inconsistent, they can suddenly become uninterested in lifelong friendships and walk away from people who were once dear to them.

Relationships

Intellectual stimuli are essential for a Gemini, so if you are paired with this sign, you must keep your relationship fresh and interesting. Gemini are attracted to intelligence and will not be swayed by good looks if a person isn't smart. They often have more than one marriage because of their need for change, so someone who understands their multiple personalities will be better suited to them. They are not always happy settling in one place or with one partner, so if you are compulsive or have no need for stability, then this sign is for you!

Moonlight Meditation

Using the let-it-go power of the waning moon, Gemini can focus on shedding the negative energy that takes hold of their spirit, leading to anxiety and worry:

On a waning moon, before sleep, speak this incantation repeatedly:

"I offer up gratitude for my ability to enjoy life.
I seek the wisdom to keep worry at bay, to prevent it
from entering my psyche, so that I may share more
of my positive energy with the people I love."

CANCER

June 21–July 22

WATER SIGN

RULING PLANET: **MOON**
SYMBOLIC COLOR: **INDIGO, YELLOW**
GEMSTONE: **MOONSTONE**
PLANT: **MOONWORT**

"If anything is worth doing,
do it with all your heart."—BUDDHA

Positive Traits

CANCERS are the empaths of the zodiac, who have big hearts and show love to those around them. A Cancer is the kind of friend who looks out for you, takes you out for a fun night, and keeps you laughing. Their imaginations are beyond compare, and they have a great sense of loyalty to their loved ones. When you befriend a Cancer, you will have a friend for life. Family is all-important to them, so they make compassionate wives, husbands, and parents.

Negative Traits

Cancer's downside is that they have extremely active imaginations that can take hold and cause jealousy and insecurities. As a result, they are inclined to portray manipulative behaviors. For example, if a coworker is undermining them, they may panic and start dropping hints to the boss that this person is not all they're cracked up to be.

Often, they do not let go of the past while simultaneously showing anxiety over the future. Cancer folk tends to worry about that which has not yet happened.

Relationships

The jealous Cancer in a relationship may snoop or accuse their partner of wrongdoing. They know this behavior is wrong but feel powerless to stop their actions in those moments.

For the most part, though, Cancer is a stable, affectionate, and extremely loyal partner. They are a light in the darkness and warmth in the cold.

Moonlight Meditation

Cancer's tendency toward jealousy is a torment not only for their friends and partners but for themselves, too. For their moonlight meditation, Cancer may concentrate on bidding farewell to envy for good.

On a waning moon, before sleep, speak this incantation repeatedly:

"May I learn to let go of
insecurities that come to me.
May I have the strength and confidence
to trust in my own abilities and to release
the urge to act out in negative ways."

LEO

July 23–August 22

FIRE SIGN

RULING PLANET: **SUN**
SYMBOLIC COLOR: **YELLOW, ORANGE**
GEMSTONE: **TIGER'S EYE**
PLANT: **SUNFLOWER**

"Joy is a net of love by which you can catch sould."—MOTHER TERESA

Positive Traits

A **Leo** has the heart of a lion and, like Gemini, is the life and soul of any party. This is a person who revels in the spotlight and drinks up any attention he or she can get. Leos are charismatic and love to enjoy themselves in any situation, whether at home, at work, on vacation, in the grocery store—anywhere, anytime! This person will lead the charge, push the envelope, and encourage others to join in the raucous festivities.

They are vivacious, confident, and usually successful in most goals they set their mind to achieving. Leos are loyal. They make great friends and love to share the joy with others. In fact, Leo is a party-thrower and known for bringing people together.

Negative Traits

Because Leos have larger-than-life personalities, they can regularly come across as self-centered and shallow. They are closed to criticism and can become annoyingly detached from compassion.

Leo is also one of the most materialistic signs of the zodiac. Those with this sign can be insensitive to others not as fortunate as them. Many Leos can be set in their ways and impulsive, whereas shy or quieter Leos are sometimes described as more sensitive.

Relationships

Leos can often be consumed with jealously and need a lot of reassurance to know their partner loves them. When they do feel secure in their relationships, they are warm and loving individuals. Leos appreciate honesty so will always like to discuss everything with their mate.

Moonlight Meditation

Leos are full of life and love and can be true delights. They can also be blind to others' suffering. This sign can ask to increase their empathetic side during meditation.

On a waxing moon, before sleep, speak this incantation repeatedly:

"I give gratitude for the friends and family I love.
I seek to grow my empathy,
so that I may respond to my loved ones' pain.
I seek to be a comfort to those I love,
in good times and in bad."

VIRGO

August 23–September 22

EARLY SIGN

RULING PLANET: **MERCURY**
SYMBOLIC COLOR: **BROWN**
GEMSTONE: **OPAL**
PLANT: **ALOE**

---

*"We are what we repeatedly do. Excellence, then,
is not an act, but a habit."* —WILL DURANT

Positive Traits

When you meet a **VIRGO**, you meet someone who walks very deliberately through life. Virgos are known for their work ethic, kindness, and loving nature. They are supposedly the most intelligent sign of the zodiac, but they come across as shy or unsure of themselves, even though they appear to be at the head of the class.

Virgos make wonderful artists, musicians, writers, and painters. They are prone to be worker bees, to the point where they just can't see how good their own work is. They are unparalleled in their focus on goals and their loyalty to loved ones. Many Virgos would do well to give themselves a break now and then. Our advice to Virgos: ease up on the perfectionism and learn to balance hard work with an adequate amount of rest and fun.

Negative Traits

Because the sign of Virgo is a mix of hard work and emotion, it can be very difficult for even a Virgo's closest friends to convince them that their achievements are out of this world. Self-doubt is a major factor in their personalities, and it's hard to convince them otherwise—their timidity is no act. They are sensitive and fragile and do not do well in confrontational situations. A lack of self-confidence will rear its head all through a Virgo's life.

Relationships

At times Virgos can be a little controlling of their partner, but this stems from a fear of losing them. They are caring and loving and need lots of attention and nurturing in return. They have a practical approach when choosing a life partner, and emotion doesn't always come into the decision-making process. When you are loved by a Virgo, they will obsessively do everything they can to please you as their other half.

Moonlight Meditation

No one will ever be as hard on a Virgo as they are on themselves. They can use the power of moonlight meditation to focus on being inwardly kind.

On a waxing moon, before sleep, speak this incantation repeatedly:

"I seek the wisdom to not only embrace
my creative and spiritual gifts
but to recognize that my power lies
in being kind to myself, so that I may refresh
my spirit and continue my work."

LIBRA

September 23–October 22

AIR SIGN

RULING PLANET: **VENUS**
SYMBOLIC COLOR: **PURPLE, GREEN**
GEMSTONE: **EMERALD**
PLANT: **ROSE**

**"The highest form of human excellence
is to question oneself and others."** —SOCRATES

Positive Traits

The scales of justice represent this sign, and true to form, **LIBRA** is interested in justice and balance. Libra is the type of person who befriends the underdog, looks out for the poor and weak, and chases away bullies. A Libra doesn't need to be personally involved in a situation to feel that it is unjust and in need of rectification, and they certainly aren't afraid to dive right into the fray. This is not to say that Libras value confrontation—quite the opposite. Most Libras would like nothing more than for the world to turn peacefully, without the need for their intervention. They have a sense of fair play, which makes them a natural leader.

Negative Traits

Libras can become frustrated with life's inequity, so any injustice will drive them through the roof. This confrontational quality is not something easily resolved through conversation. Beware, for Libras can bear malice and hold a grudge. They would do well to learn how to forgive and forget, as this trait can lead to a string of failed relationships. At times, they can be unreliable and flaky, leaving others annoyed.

Relationships

A Libra will never settle for a superficial relationship. They love with passion but are fussy when it comes to finding a mate. Because they tend toward vanity, personal appearance is key; they could become obsessed with the way their partner looks. When they finally settle into a relationship, they expect longevity and will be loyal and trustworthy.

Moonlight Meditation

Libras tend to be classic grudge-holders, a trait that leads to unhappiness for themselves and their loved ones. Libras can ask for the wisdom to forgive and forget.

On a waxing moon, before sleep, speak this incantation repeatedly:

*"I seek the strength to allow myself
to release grievances and to forgive
without settling old scores.
By doing this, I wish to increase
my sense of peace."*

SCORPIO

October 23–November 21

WATER SIGN

RULING PLANET: **MARS**
SYMBOLIC COLOR: **RED, BLUE, GREEN**
GEMSTONE: **RUBY**
PLANT: **IVY, OAK**

**"One can never consent to creep when
one feels the impulse to soar."** —HELEN KELLER

Positive Traits

One of the psychic signs of the zodiac, SCORPIOS can sometimes
have a spiritual approach to life. They are passionate about
their interests, ultrafocused, and motivated to do well.
Whether in business, the arts, fitness, relationships, or
recreation, these folks go hard at everything, and it
shows. A Scorpio has a strong personality type and
usually say exactly what is on their mind. Honesty is
the best policy, and they never sugarcoat. Scorpios are
people you want on your team if you are planning a big
project, like building a house or launching a business.

Their attention to detail is outstanding, and they don't quit until things are done the right way.

Negative Traits

The downside of all this passion is that Scorpios can have something of a bad temper. Patience is not their strong suit, especially in their younger years, and temper tantrums (even of the adult variety) are not uncommon. A jealous Scorpio is a formidable person, as they will stop at nothing to put themselves back in the limelight.

Scorpios can work on taming emotions when they get out of control in the form of anger, jealousy, or impatience. Because, while a little of this ferocity can be productive, too much of it may prove to be destructive in countless ways.

Relationships

Watch out for the tail's venomous stinger! A Scorpio cannot accept betrayal in love and will turn vengeful. When they do "click" with someone, they automatically become a protector type and will strive for a commitment that you won't find in any other sign. Scorpios love physical intimacy and have very few inhibitions. Bouncing off the bedposts and swinging on the chandeliers is usual for this birth sign. They show love through intimacy and enjoy the pleasures of the flesh.

Moonlight Meditation

Scorpios are hard-working and industrious but often lacks patience. In their meditation, Scorpios can concentrate on increasing tolerance levels. On a waxing moon, before sleep, speak this incantation repeatedly:

*"I give gratitude for having a true passion for my work,
my friends, and my family. Let me focus my efforts now
on developing a more patient nature, that I may be kind
in every situation, even when I am frustrated."*

SAGITTARIUS
November 22–December 21

FIRE SIGN

RULING PLANET: **JUPITER**
SYMBOLIC COLOR: **PURPLE, BLUE, WHITE**
GEMSTONE: **TOPAZ**
PLANT: **SAGE**

"**Adopt the pace of nature: her secret is patience.**"
—RALPH WALDO EMERSON

Positive Traits

This sign longs for the freedom to do what they want without being held back. **SAGITTARIANS** are free spirits, and travel is a big part of that. They love new experiences and feeling as though they are the first person to accomplish something—whether it be climbing a mountain, forging a river, or conquering their chosen field of work. Make no mistake, though—these folks aren't hermits who hide out in the woods. They are achievers in their own right, determined to blaze their own trail, the sort who will make a career out of being a wilderness guide, ski instructor, or charter boat captain. The usual nine-to-five desk job is tough for the Sagittarian, as they spend their time calculating how many minutes are left in the workday until they can get outside. Sagittarians are also known for being extremely personable. They get along with everyone and are often the unelected leaders of any given group. They don't seek the spotlight but are happy to use their powers for the good of the many.

Negative Traits

This sign can sometimes lose focus, partly due to their need to feel unconstrained and partly due to their extremely idealistic nature. Dreaminess and impatience can combine to turn this generally genial sign into an outspoken and irritable person. This is not their normal state, but it is a tendency worth recognizing and working to tame. They can often show signs of being petty and grumpy in later life. Occasionally you will come across a Sagittarian who has a bit of an ego, always wanting to be right and fixed in their opinions.

Relationships

A Sagittarian will not be happy in a mundane marriage and dislikes nothing more than a monotonous routine. They should seek a partner who brings adventure or who can at least support them in their adventuring. They are not typically romantic, which can often lead to their spouse feeling neglected, so it is usually the case that a Sagittarian will have more than one marriage. However, they are typically faithful and, because they have a love of freedom, will not restrict their partner from having outside interests or separate friendships.

Moonlight Meditation

A Sagittarius is a genial sign who tends to feel constrained by schedules and official responsibilities. This person can use the full moon's power to help quiet urges to ditch their duties when it's a perfect day for hiking or skiing.

On a full moon, before sleep, speak this incantation repeatedly:

"I express gratitude for the wonder of nature and my love of the outdoors.
I seek a balance between my desire to be outside
and the tasks I am required to do."

CAPRICORN

December 22–January 19

EARTH SIGN

RULING PLANET: **SATURN**
SYMBOLIC COLOR: **BLACK, VIOLET, GREEN**
GEMSTONE: **GARNET**
PLANT: **WEEPING WILLOW**

"Be the leader you would follow."—UNKNOWN

Positive Traits

CAPRICORN is your grown-up friend, the one who is grounded and responsible and tries to make the right choices most of the time. These are probably the hardest workers of the zodiac and make for wonderful providers. For these reasons, this sign produces great leaders. Capricorns have innately careful personalities and tend to lean toward rational, well-thought-out decisions. Just as importantly, this sign will admit their mistakes and make an effort not to repeat them. Capricorn accepts that there is room for improvement in their methods and seeks to be a better person, leader, parent, and friend.

Negative Traits

With all of the positives going on, what kind of shortcomings could this sign have? Capricorns can be rigid in their beliefs and opinions and revert to what is most familiar and comfortable. This means that a Capricorn may be reluctant to dive into new experiences or meet new people. And once a Capricorn feels out of sorts, a negative attitude can take hold, which can lead to depression in later life. Capricorns would do well to recognize these feelings when they start to emerge. Conquering this tendency can open the door to new experiences that will only serve Capricorn well.

Relationships

Because they are steadfast and reliable, Capricorns need a partner who has the same characteristics of being highly moral and independent. They will not give their heart freely and, even when married, can sometimes be cold or unfeeling. Once you break a Capricorn's walls down and they learn to trust and bond, they are sensitive and protective partners. Love tends to blossom over time with this sign.

Moonlight Meditation

Capricorn is kind and generous but may also be close-minded at times. Capricorn can use meditation to focus on welcoming new situations as they arise.

On a waxing moon, before sleep, speak this incantation repeatedly:

*"Allow me the wisdom to recognize
that I have more to learn in this life.
When new people enter my circle,
I wish to be welcoming. I want to be open to
new experiences and to seek the lessons in them."*

AQUARIUS

January 20–February 18

AIR SIGN

RULING PLANET: **SATURN**
SYMBOLIC COLOR: **YELLOW, VIOLET, WHITE**
GEMSTONE: **TOPAZ AND SAPPHIRE**
PLANT: **BIRD OF PARADISE**

"One must still have chaos in oneself to be able to give birth to a dancing star."—FRIEDRICH NIETZSCHE

Positive Traits

AQUARIANS love their alone time. They not only enjoy solitude but crave it. These people are creative, intelligent, and completely original who need time by themselves to ground and recharge. Without this opportunity, Aquarians can become temperamental and moody.

Because Aquarians are always thinking outside of the box, so to speak, they have an enlightened quality and a vision that is best described as almost ethereal. These folks struggle to comingle this element of their personality with the reality of living in the everyday world. They are constantly seeking to tweak their creative edge while succeeding in personal, unique ways. Aquarians are loving, generous individuals who also cultivate friendships well. They are never boring and are wonderful communicators.

Negative Traits

Aquarians often have their heads in the clouds and often slip into daydreams. The sign of the water bearer is an emotional one, so they can frequently become frustrated with global matters. Their weakness is that they become disconnected with the world they live in and can feel detached from people around them. Because they think outside of the box, they are prone to being eccentric. An Aquarius will never forget, so if you upset one, they will remind you of your past mistakes for years to come. Constructive criticism doesn't sit well with them, either.

Relationships

An Aquarius needs to be swept off their feet and have a devoted partner for life. They crave a soulmate and won't accept anything less. They need a lot of reassurance that the bond is strong, so this sign would not suit a more laid-back spouse. They can be argumentative by nature and take the more dominant role, yet they are truly loyal and very caring, especially if their partner is going through hardships. A sense of humor is a vital characteristic for Aquarians, as they have a lovely sense of fun about them.

Moonlight Meditation

Aquarians are often torn between wanting to belong and knowing that their talents set them completely apart from others. Using the influence of the waxing moon, an Aquarius can focus on increasing a sense of harmony by learning to accept themselves.

On a waxing moon, before sleep, speak this incantation repeatedly:

"Let me express gratitude for my unique abilities,
that I may recognize them for the gifts they are. I seek peace
in knowing it's all right for me to be different from others and to
follow my own path on the way to my version of success."

PISCES

February 19–March 20

WATER SIGN

RULING PLANET: **NEPTUNE**
SYMBOLIC COLOR: **BLUE, AZURE, GREEN**
GEMSTONE: **AMETHYST AND ONYX**
PLANT: **LOTUS**

"No act of kindness, no matter how small,
is ever wasted."—AESOP

Positive Traits

The final sign of the zodiac, **PISCES** is a wise and thoughtful observer of the world. Kind and patient, these folks are accepting of all kinds of personality types and often overlook the hurtful actions of others as they seek to understand their behavior rather than judge it.

This is one of the most sensitive and creative signs of the zodiac. Pisces enjoy escaping reality and tend to enjoy immersing themselves in reading, writing, music, and nature. If you are born under this sign, you are more than likely psychic or clairvoyant in some way. Astrologers identify Pisces as being the most psychic sign in the zodiac.

Negative Traits

Pisces is also known for being a classic daydreamer, someone with big ideas who gets so wrapped up in their thoughts that they never get around to taking the steps necessary to bring them to fruition.

They can also be pessimistic and overanalyze to the point of anxiety. Criticism of any kind can shut a Pisces down for days, but they can learn to overcome their fears by facing them head-on instead of withdrawing into solitude. Sometimes referred to as "victims," Pisces would do well to accept that some people in the world will not treat others as well as they should. In these cases it is best to let go of the relationship when appropriate to do so. Pisces are a submissive type who are easily influenced.

Relationships

Pisces need a lot of romance in their life, so they will seek a soulmate who is completely devoted to them and will indulge them in every way. They are usually attracted to water signs like Scorpio or Cancer, as their fellow water signs will be more likely to understand a Pisces' feelings and emotions. Pisces have a strong faith in people and can often attract damaged individuals or folks with deep-seated, emotional baggage. Their love of love can often lead them into disruptive relationships that will leave them having little or no self-confidence when it comes around to finding love again. They are not demanding partners, but instead are attentive listeners and will always aim to please. Pisceans have faith in love, even after many romantic disappointments.

Moonlight Meditation

Pisces tend to get wrapped up in their own heads and take any hint of criticism too much to heart. Under the light of a waxing moon, Pisces can focus on increasing a sense of confidence, by speaking this incantation repeatedly before sleep:

"I give gratitude for having a sensitive nature. I now seek to feel self-assured about my abilities so that I may share them more freely with others."

Part Three

DIVINATION
MAGICK

Chapter 11

The Art of Divination

FROM EGYPT AND GREECE TO HINDUS AND HEBREWS, throughout time each culture has had its own form of divination, or the art of plugging into the universal life force to gain insight and knowledge. You might be looking for the answer to a very specific question, or maybe you want more general information. Whatever the query is, there is a form of foretelling that will lead you to a reply.

There are literally countless methods of divination, with most originating in ancient cultures. Centuries ago, folk interpreted cloud formations or read the dust on tables, or by studying candles, bones, or even fingernails.

Some divination techniques seem lost to time, but many witches sustained their practice through the centuries. In this chapter we discuss some of the more common forms of divination.

Those of you exploring new methods of divination, keep in mind that this subject is vast; we cannot list all practices. Information on more obscure practices is readily available online. In this chapter we cover the basics of divination in the forms of reading bones, studying the body, observing the skies, using pendulums, burning candles, reading palms, and scrying reflective surfaces, and we mention other forms of divination along the way.

BONE TOSSING

Reading bones, or *osteomancy*, is a means of divination dating back to ancient China. In days of yore, Chinese seers consulted with the rich and powerful, whose questions varied from whether war or famine was coming to which spirit might be causing their ailments or had wiped out their livestock. In Asia, modern archeologists and historians have uncovered large quantities of turtle shells and singular animal bones engraved with cryptic writing.

Ancient diviners often used tortoise plastrons (the large belly covering) or the scapulas of oxen or other large animals for bone readings, as the relatively flat surfaces of these pieces made the job of question-and-answer a bit easier. The bones were cleaned of meat and then prepared with various tools to make their already-flat shape even flatter. Holes were drilled into the bones in a methodical fashion.

The diviner would etch a question onto its surface. Then, using a rod or other means, heat was applied to a pit or a drilled hole until the bone cracked. The resulting pieces were interpreted by the diviner, and often the answer was etched in the bone afterward as well.

This method of bone divination differs slightly from the more modern practice you may be familiar with, which includes collecting a variety of bones, throwing them, and interpreting how they land. Casting bones in this manner is widely practiced today.

Where to Find Bones

Modern bone readers often use possum bones to connect with the spiritual plane and interpret its messages. Possums are believed to have a strong connection with the dead, as they are nocturnal animals sometimes seen roaming cemeteries in the dark. However, chickens have been used in sacrifices and rituals in African American hoodoo and African voodoo for many years, which indicates that this animal also has a powerful tie to the ancestral world. As chicken bones may be more readily available, they are a good choice for this form of divination.

Osteomancy is like many other methods of divination—it's highly personal. Standard osteomancy kits can be purchased online or from New Age shops, but while kits are a good start, it's preferable to use bones with which you have a personal connection. Some bone collectors say that using bones from roadkill gives them a stronger bond and better reading, as they:

- **Know where the bones came from**
- **Know something about how the animal died**
- **Can personally clean the bones**
- **Can honor the animal and give it a proper burial**

However, not everyone gets excited about the idea of harvesting bones from dead animals. So for those, like us, who tend to be a little squeamish, there are other options. Whether you buy them or find them, keep your bones together in a satchel or cloth. Add some additional objects that have personal significance to you, such as seashells, feathers, stones, pieces of bark, or even your own trinkets (keys, a loose earring, coins). This could be anything, as long as it's small enough to fit in the bag and toss with the bones, and as long as it holds special meaning.

Reading Bones

There are a couple of methods for this type of reading, depending on which kind of bones you're using. If you purchase a kit and/or are using the mixed-bone method, it will include some standard pieces like a scapula, a tooth, a raccoon penile bone, and chicken wing bones. Other bones are included based on availability.

For example, they might represent:

- **Past**
- **Present**
- **Future**
- **Obstacles**

. . . . or they may signify home, career, relationships, and health. Any other combination you come up with is suitable.

MIXED-BONE METHOD [definition]

Back in the olden days, diviners would draw a circle in the dirt, divided into four quadrants, and cast bones there. Nowadays most people use some sort of fabric as a casting surface, with the simplest option being a humble piece of cloth. Some use animal hide, and others use a special cloth with a preprinted circle divided into four quadrants. No matter which textile you opt for, you must be sure to divide the casting area into four quadrants. You can define these sections based on the reading you are performing.

If you're using a plain cloth, decide before casting your stones how you will interpret their layout. Will objects that land closest to you be representative of current events, or will they speak to the past? Will you read the objects in a linear fashion at all, or will you read their layout as a big picture of events? Any bone or trinket that lands off of the cloth (or outside of your circular grid) will not be used in the reading at all.

Here's where your personal connection to the bones and other objects comes into play. Let's say you're using a bone that you found while walking in the woods. Before you found that bone, you were feeling melancholy, but after your discovery, you felt completely engaged with the nature around you. With this experience in mind, maybe that bone signifies redemption or rebirth for you. Before you start your reading, assign meaning to each object and bone in your collection so that you can interpret their presentation accordingly.

Keep a notebook of what the objects in your collection mean to you. Remember, this can be a fluid relationship: today, maybe an acorn indicates growth, but next year it might represent something entirely different for reasons that are unknown to you now. That is okay as long as you take the time to connect with your bone-throwing collection on a regular basis, to infuse it with your own energy.

Tossing Chicken Bones

Chicken bones have some standard meanings, according to old-time readers. It is perfectly fine to use the bones of a chicken that you have eaten for dinner. Boil the bird to get the remaining meat off and remove the bones you'll be using for divination. (You may want to soak them in dish soap for a few days to get all the grease off). Once they are cleaned, soak them in peroxide (not bleach, as this will break down the bones) for a day or two to brighten them. Remove and dry, and they are ready for use. Some people paint their bones; some use them as they are.

Note that only seven bones can be used from an entire hen. Their meanings are below:

BREASTBONE Love, relationships, artistic endeavors, and passion in life and love

LEG BONE, BROKEN Delays, hindrances, isolation, frustration

LEG BONE, WHOLE Land travel, potential realized, opening opportunities

NECKBONE Scarcity in resources, loss, anxiety, poor decisions

RIB BONE Restrictions, obstacles, difficulties to overcome

THIGH BONE Spirituality, emotional trials, ancestors, spiritual gifts

WING BONE, BROKEN Freedom curtailed, being stuck, delays

WING BONE, WHOLE Freedom, air travel, possibilities, future improvement

WISHBONE Hopes, aspirations, dreams coming true, luck

Toss your chicken bones and notice how they land in relation to one another. There are some shapes the bones will take that may clue you into messages:

DIAGONAL LINE Separation as it relates to the bones around it

HORIZONTAL LINE Represents feminine energy; indicates a negative response

HORSESHOE Represents luck, unless it's upside-down, which represents negative energy

PARALLEL TO ONE ANOTHER The energies are in agreement

T-SHAPE One bone is blocking the energy of the other

UPRIGHT TRIANGLE Growth in a positive direction

UPSIDE-DOWN TRIANGLE Diminishing energy or growth

VERTICAL LINE Represents masculine energy, indicates a positive response

X-SHAPE Working together or against one another

As with any kind of divination, practice makes perfect. You need to throw the bones regularly to understand the relationship of the bones to one another, as well as their connection to your mind and spirit.

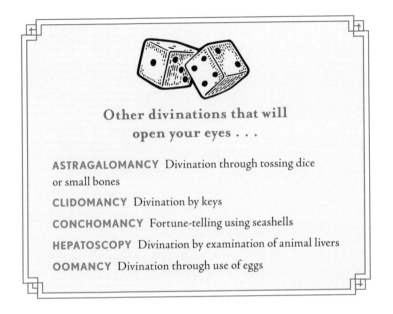

Other divinations that will open your eyes . . .

ASTRAGALOMANCY Divination through tossing dice or small bones

CLIDOMANCY Divination by keys

CONCHOMANCY Fortune-telling using seashells

HEPATOSCOPY Divination by examination of animal livers

OOMANCY Divination through use of eggs

DIVINING USING THE BODY

There are several means of reading characteristics of or on the human body. For instance, *moleomancy* is the practice of interpreting birthmarks and moles to determine a person's fate as well as their true personality. Though it has its roots in ancient times, this form of divination is rather rare these days.

Birthmarks are often given higher regard than moles, but the interpretation of either is often quite literal, depending on your source and beliefs. For example, a mole on the forehead may indicate high intelligence and an unusually high level of creativity. A mole on the calf may signal someone is destined to travel great distances. A birthmark on the hip may indicate trouble in the joints, and so on. (Note: If, during an examination of your own body for moles, you notice moles that are large, irregular in color, or asymmetrical, or that have changed over time, please consult with a dermatologist.)

Some other, less literal interpretation of moles:

ABDOMEN, LOWER Person will regularly fail to deliver on promises

ABDOMEN, UPPER Discomfort with appearance and/or personality

BACK, NEAR SPINAL COLUMN Truthfulness and sincerity, well-liked and popular

BACK, LEFT Daring, brave, determined

BACK, RIGHT Tact, discretion, peacekeeper

CALF, LEFT Extensive travel and worldwide connections

CALF, RIGHT Accomplishments, achievement, success

CHEEK, LEFT Egotism, aloofness, overconfidence

CHEEK, RIGHT Kindness, loyalty, duty

CHEST, CENTER Money troubles will plague this person

CHEST, LEFT Intelligence coupled with social anxiety

CHEST, RIGHT Person will have female children

CHIN, CENTER Hails from nobility or royalty and commands great respect

CHIN, LEFT No-nonsense communicator, wasteful spender

CHIN, CHIN, RIGHT Logical, balanced, wise

FOOT, LEFT Poor marriage with family troubles

FOOT, RIGHT Good marriage, devoted to family and higher power

HAND, LEFT Tries hard but experiences many letdowns

HAND, RIGHT Fortitude, grit, determination

NOSE, CENTER Poor health

NOSE, LEFT Dishonest and decadent

NOSE, RIGHT Effortless earnings and wealth

PHILTRUM Higher-than-average sex drive

THIGH, LEFT Artistic expression and talent

THIGH, RIGHT Bravery, extensive travel

WRIST, RIGHT OR LEFT Financial hardships in youth that will turn around in middle age

According to some forms of astrology, the placement of moles and birthmarks on the body can tell you about the influence of the planets when the person was in their mother's womb. Markings on the left side of the body indicate that the planets were exerting a feminine influence; markings on the right side of the body tell of a male influence. The color of a mole adds another layer of classification. Black moles are bad luck, while virtually any other color denotes good fortune. (Your dermatologist may or may not agree.) Some witches believe that a mole in this life is a wound or mark from a previous life and that you can carry these scars on your body from one life to the next.

There are many websites devoted to mole interpretation, so if you don't see a specific marking noted in this chapter, don't fret. Chances are high that it is defined somewhere in cyberspace.

More Body Reading

Physiognomy is a means of identifying personality traits by reading features of the face and head. Philosophers like Aristotle and Hippocrates endorsed its validity, asserting that many facial features are linked to gestation and medical conditions and therefore do indeed provide insight into personality and potential.

Some examples of physiognomy interpretations:

ATTACHED EARLOBES Dominant to the point of bullying

CLOSE-SET EYES Shrewd insight concerning the world and relationships

CROOKED NOSE "Wandering eye"; chaos in personal relationships

FAR-SET EYES Naïve and intolerant of surprises but quite loving

FULL LIPS Expressive and honest, holds nothing back

LONG CANINE TEETH Considered a "jinx," bringing bad luck to those around them

NARROW NOSE Self-reliant and private

POINTY CHIN Highly sensitive, takes things personally, oppositional

PROMINENT EARS Independence, intelligence, and creative thought

PROTRUDING EYES Assertive and overconfident at times

SHORT NOSE Worrier, defeatist, depressed personality

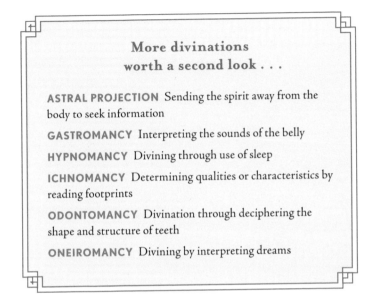

**More divinations
worth a second look . . .**

ASTRAL PROJECTION Sending the spirit away from the body to seek information

GASTROMANCY Interpreting the sounds of the belly

HYPNOMANCY Divining through use of sleep

ICHNOMANCY Determining qualities or characteristics by reading footprints

ODONTOMANCY Divination through deciphering the shape and structure of teeth

ONEIROMANCY Divining by interpreting dreams

THIN LIPS Standoffish but honest, guarded and vigilant

UNDERSIZE CHIN Unambitious, cautious to a fault, avoids confrontation at all costs

UNIBROW Intense worry, self-consciousness

VERTICAL LINES ON EARLOBES Health problems, weak constitution

WIDE NOSE Loving, family-oriented, generous beyond compare

Of course, so many people have plastic surgery these days that it might be tough to determine which parts are real and which are enhanced. One thing to know for sure is that although surgery may alter one's appearance, the personality traits remain the same.

GET YOUR HEAD IN THE CLOUDS

Who doesn't love watching big puffy clouds make their way across a summer sky, or storm clouds rolling in on the horizon? Did you know there is a way to discern the future from weather observations? This is a form of divination called *aeromancy*, and it involves the interpretation of clouds, currents, and the cosmos. (Just the thing for those of us who walk around with our head in the proverbial clouds all the time.)

Aeromancy allows the reader to connect with information from a higher source. The most important factor, as with any form of divination, is having the ability to clear your mind and receive and interpret incoming

messages. It's especially important with aeromancy, because an agitated or overloaded mind just won't be able to see images in the clouds.

In order to have a successful aeromany session, choose a day when reading different cloud formations will be possible. While you can really do this during many forms of weather, it's going to be very difficult to read clouds if the sky is a sheet of overcast gray with no visible differentiation in cloud forms. Find a comfortable spot where you can recline or lie flat on your back. Try to choose a place where there isn't a lot of foot traffic or excessive noise. If headphones and white noise or relaxing music help you clear your mind, use them.

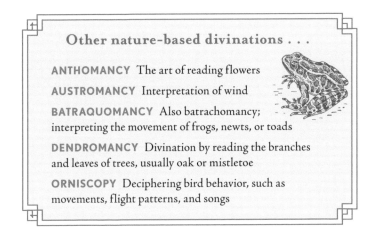
Start by meditating, perhaps by saying or thinking something like, *"I ask to be free from judgment. I wish to enter into this session with an open state of mind, an open heart, and creative insight. I ask that this be granted to me."* Breathe deeply and get yourself into a state of relaxation. Focus on your question with your eyes closed.

Now open your eyes. Let the cloud forms appear as whatever your mind wants them to be: faces, letters, numbers, animals, otherworldly beings—there's no limit. Close your eyes again and meditate on how these images relate to your question. Repeat the exercise if you feel inclined. Once you feel an answer may have been reached, write down the images in a journal. Some of the images may not make sense to you immediately, but they may ring a bell in a day or two.

That's it. You've had time to relax and observe the beauty of nature, and hopefully you've received the information you were looking for along the way.

PENDULUM POWER

Pellomancy, or divination through use of a pendulum, can be a lot of fun, but it does take some practice. As you likely know, a pendulum consists of some sort of weighted material that hangs from a chain or a string. The pendulum can be used to answer yes or no questions, or, if you are seeking more involved communication, you can create a chart with a variety of answers and allow the pendulum to swing toward the correct choice.

Some people want to know if the weight needs to be made from a specific material, like a crystal. You can certainly do this, but it's not necessary. What is most important is your connection with the universe and the pendulum itself; something we will talk about shortly. If you are interested in using a crystal for your pendulum weight, here are some good options:

AMETHYST, OBSIDIAN, and LAPIS LAZULI Foster psychic energy, balance, and peace

CITRINE Promotes abundance and prosperity

FLUORITE Encourages a clear and organized mind

HEMATITE Contains grounding properties; offers protection from negative energies

HONEY CALCITE and RUBY Stimulate positive energy for personal goals

ROSE QUARTZ Boosts healing energies, both physical and emotional

SELENITE Helps with psychic energy and mental clarity

SMOKY QUARTZ Wards off negative energy; promotes grounding and prosperity

There is an abundance of crystals to choose from. If the descriptions above do not speak to you, you can search the Internet for a crystal that aligns with your personal needs. You can also use a pendulum made of stone or metal. Test out different sizes, shapes, and weights (do this for crystals, too, if you use them) to determine what feels most comfortable to you. Some people prefer to work with a large weight, while others prefer a weight that is much smaller. This is a very personal choice, so don't feel obliged to choose a pendulum exactly like the one your friend has.

Some pendulums come on a very long chain. This can make people with shorter arms feel as though they really can't interpret what the weight is doing, because it's simply hanging too low. Gather up as much of the chain as needed in order to read the movements of the pendulum.

Start by sitting at a table and stabilizing your elbow on the surface. Begin to physically move your pendulum forward and backward. When it is in full swing, ask it which direction means "yes." It might start moving in a clockwise direction, so you will know that is your answer. Next, ask it the sign for "no" and then "I don't know."

Some will swing back and forth to indicate a positive or negative answer and then come to a dead stop to indicate the opposite. This is a time to observe and learn about your pendulum's behavior. If you are a collector of pendulums, don't expect every one of them to be the same. You will need to establish these yes and no movements with each pendulum you own.

Get to know your pendulum by asking some rudimentary questions. Come up with some questions to which you know the answers, making sure those answers are black and white, yes or no.

Some simple introductory questions might include:

- **Is my name Mary?**

- **Is it daytime?**

- **Is it summertime?**

- **Do I have a dog?**

- **Am I at home right now?**

- **Is red my favorite color?**

If you receive unclear responses from your pendulum, contemplate whether you can rephrase the question in a simpler manner.

Now that you have an idea of how to use a pendulum, think of some areas in your life where you'd like to gain clarity. Brainstorm ways to phrase these questions clearly and specifically. Examples of clearly phrased questions:

- **Will I get the job I interviewed for yesterday?**

- **Will I be promoted at work within six months?**

- **Will I get married within the next twelve months?**

- **Should I travel on Thursday?**

- **Is now a good time to adopt a pet?**

- **Will my health improve this year?**

- **Should I buy the blue house I looked at last week?**

- **Will I find a significant other within three months?**

Again, your questions should be highly personal to what is happening in your life. If you can add a specific time frame, you may find clearer answers. For example, "Should I travel this week?" is sort of specific but also somewhat open-ended. If you are driving three hours to attend a meeting for work and you have a choice to leave on either Thursday or Friday, your pendulum may give you an indication that one day will be hassle-free while the other may be heavy with traffic or slowed by inclement weather.

Important Points to Remember

- **Ask one question at a time.** Don't ask, "*Should I adopt a dog or cat?*" In a situation like this, break that into two questions.

- **Do not make it overly complicated.** Simplify the question "*Should I bring a coat tonight because it might rain?*" into either "*Should I take a coat with me tonight?*" or "*Is it going to rain tonight?*"

- **Try to phrase questions in a positive light.** Change "*Did I make the wrong choice in the car I bought?*" to "*Did I make the right decision in buying my new car?*"

- **After you've determined the meanings of your pendulums movements,** don't continue asking questions to which you already know the answers. This is game-playing and can lead to confusing results due to your own mixed-up energy!

Going Further

To gain insight into more involved questions, you can create a chart populated with possible appropriate responses. Pie charts tend to work best, as they give the pendulum a central starting point and easy access to every potential answer. Should you have three job offers on the table and want to know which is the best fit, you would draw a pie chart with each option represented as an equal slice. Leave a small circle in the center of the chart as a neutral starting point.

Decide what kind of information you want.

- **Which job should you take?**
- **Which company will present the most opportunity for your career?**
- **Which company will have the most relaxed atmosphere?**
- **Which job will feel most rewarding?**

You might also be entranced by . . .

ACULTOMANCY Reading the swinging of a needle

BELOMANCY Divination by balancing or throwing arrows, or by drawing them out of a container

BIBLIOMANCY Divination by use of books, especially the Bible

DACTYLIOMANCY Fortune-telling using rings

LITHOMANCY Interpretation of precious stones, charms, or talismans

---

Using a chart gives you the latitude to get more creative with your questions. The chart can contain as many pieces of information as you need. Want to know what kind of flowers you should plant? Slice your circular chart into twenty pieces if you so desire. Just make sure that you are allowing enough space for each option so you can clearly interpret your answers.

LIGHT UP YOUR FUTURE

Many people use candles in their commonplace daily routine, as aromatherapy, or as ambient light, while others plug into the spiritual side of flame by using candles as offerings or in remembrance of a loved one. You can also use candles in a couple of ways to foretell or even influence the future. Candle spells are commonplace in Wiccan traditions, and while we're going to focus on how to use candles for divination (*ceromancy*), there are many circumstances in which you just can't have one without the other.

Candle Colors

Depending on how you intend to use your candles and what information you hope to gather, you'll want to choose your color with intention. For example, for better insight on a particular day of the week:

SUNDAY Yellow

MONDAY White, silver, gray

TUESDAY Red, burgundy

WEDNESDAY Purple

THURSDAY Blue

FRIDAY Green

SATURDAY Black, purple

For divination into specific areas of inquiry:

WHITE Peace, truthfulness

GREEN Money, financial success

YELLOW Health, fertility, finances

LAVENDER, SILVER Paranormal (enhances psychic energy)

PINK Humanity, love, self-esteem, friendship

BLUE Fidelity

ORANGE Bringing plans to fruition

RED Love, sex, passionate relationships

WHITE AND BLACK Protection from and destruction of dark energies

Now that you've determined what candle color is appropriate, here's where spells, intention, and candle reading can work together. Let's say you have your eye on an attractive neighbor and you'd like to draw that person's romantic attention your way. Here's what to do:

1. Choose a red or pink candle, which represents your romantic interest.

2. Write or carve the person's name and the date you'd like to be a couple (say, two weeks from the current date) on the candle (or on the glass if it's in a container).

3. **Anoint the candle with vegetable oil or an essential oil associated with the matter at hand.** (For a list of essential oils and their meanings, see pages 266–67.)

4. **Now sit for a moment and imagine yourself with this person. Picture yourself on your first date.** Where are you? What's the weather like? If you're ordering a meal, what's on your plate? What kind of conversation are the two of you having? Focus all of your positive energy into this visualization.

5. **When you have the scene set in your mind and you feel that it's absolutely going to happen, light your candle.** You can say a few words like, *"As I have seen, so it shall be."*

6. **Allow your candle to burn.** To check on how your spell or intention is progressing, you can read the candle drippings.

Reading Candle Wax

If you have a freestanding (pillar, taper, round, or square) candle, you can interpret the way the wax is melting. This form of divinaiton is a lot like tea-leaf reading: simply look for images in the wax. As the candle is actively burning, images may appear and then change completely, or images might persist or reappear. In the case of a romantic love divination, you might see a heart appear in the wax as it melts, or drippings from the candle may form to represent a house or a bride. Maybe the wax drippings will take shape in the form of another woman or man, who might represent a rival for your affections.

If you are using a candle enclosed in a container, you can read the drippings by using a bowl of cool or room-temperature water. (Make sure to use a bowl that is a different color than your wax drippings so that you can clearly see the images that form.) Simply drip some of the wax into the water and observe the shapes that show up.

As with all forms of divination, you may choose to read your results as single answers to certain questions or as part of a bigger-picture narrative.

More Candlelight Interpretations

In addition to using candle wax to peer into the future, you can also observe the way your candle burns as a whole. Studying this will help you determine whether your intentions are going to be successful or if your energy is being blocked. Let us take the same example from before, with the love interest being the focus of the divination inquiry, and imagine we're using a freestanding candle for interpretation.

The candle melts evenly, perhaps "opening up" into a flower shape. Your intention will become reality. This is an indication of your positive energy being received and returned freely, without obstruction.

The wick gets buried in the wax and goes out. Your intention is being blocked, either by negative energy or by someone's opposition to your wishes.

The entire candle melts down to one large puddle of wax. This is ideal! This means your intention is working, and it also gives you one large wax dripping to interpret.

You can also read the flame itself, which is a skill called *pyromancy*.
If the flame . . .

BURNS HIGH Your intention is backed and met with positive energy.

BURNS LOW Negative or oppositional energy is blocking your intention.

SPITS OR POPS Spirits are trying to connect with you regarding your intention.

FLICKERS EXCESSIVELY Spirits are present. Crackling or popping indicates they are trying to speak with you.

NOT EASILY EXTINGUISHED Spirits are still working with your intention. Let the flame burn a while longer.

Of course, it goes without saying that you should never leave a candle unattended and you should always use caution when working with fire. If you must leave before the candle melts completely, use a drop of water or a candle extinguisher to put the flame out. This is a sign of respect to the spirits gathered and working on your request. You can revisit the issue again using the same candle and the same technique of visualization and preparation.

You might also be interested in . . .

BOTANOMANCY Divination by burning herbs or the branches of trees

CAPNOMANCY Decoding the rising smoke from a fire

CAUSINOMANCY Seeking information by burning objects

LAMPADOMANCY Divination using an oil lamp or torch

SPODOMANCY Also known as *tephramancy*, divination by interpreting cinders, soot, or ashes

YOUR FUTURE,
IN THE PALM OF YOUR HAND

Palmistry (also called *chiromancy* or *chirosophy*), is believed to have at least some origin in the Hindu religion. Many cultures adopted palmistry, so there are different meanings in every background. Astrologer William John Warner, popularly known as Cheiro, studied with masters in India and brought a renewed popularity to the practice in Western Europe in the early twentieth century. Much of what we think of as modern palmistry is based on Cheiro's work.

Palmistry is a vast, technical subject that warrants a book all its own. It is so involved that to read a palm properly from a print or a photocopy would take many hours. Every line on your palm is like a map of your life, and because everyone's life is different, no two palms are the same. The following information is merely a bite-size chunk of some of the basics in the Western and Vedic traditions.

Hands

First you can start by assessing the size of the hand in proportion to the body type.

BIG HANDS Sensitive, creative, and naturally inquisitive, people with large hands have an eye for detail that small-handed people may miss. Big-handed folks are all about digging for answers.

MID-SIZE HANDS People with mid-size hands usually go with the flow. They don't get angry, they don't hang on to grudges, and they aren't prone to mood swings. They want peace in life and seek it out diligently.

SMALL HANDS These people are big thinkers but sometimes miss the forest for the trees. Still, these folks are achievement-oriented, focused, and determined.

Now, take a look at the shape of the hand.

THICK, SQUARE HANDS People with these hands are quite work-oriented, often workaholics. They tend not to get tangled up in too many thoughts at once because they prefer to be doing something. These folks are no-nonsense and low-emotion, and get real satisfaction out of working hard and producing something useful. Square hands belong to practical people who often work outdoors.

THIN HANDS Thin hands are indicative of a thinking person, someone who has ideas piling up in their mind. These folks are brilliant but can be quite moody, depending on where their thoughts are leading them. Even so, these people are logical and find practical solutions to problems.

Fingers

Next take a look at the fingers.

MEDIUM FINGERS These represent balance in most areas and usually belong to well-rounded individuals.

LONG FINGERS Instead of ruminating on situations and ideas, long-fingered folks tend to act without a lot of thought and sometimes find themselves in a real mess because of it. These people tend to operate on emotion and may miss important facts.

SHORT FINGERS Nimble people generally have short fingers. They are those who think and act quickly, and usually with good judgment.

Names of Fingers

Each one of the fingers, not including the thumb, is named as follows.

FOREFINGER OR INDEX–JUPITER Jupiter represents career and idealism. If this finger is long, it can mean the person may be likely to venture into self-employment; this could be anything from a small business to a chain of companies. If the Jupiter finger is shorter, it shows a lack of ambition and someone who suffers from no self-confidence.

MIDDLE FINGER–SATURN Saturn symbolizes psychology. If this finger is long, the owner likes privacy and solitude and has a love of learning. If short, this person could be regarded as thoughtless or careless.

RING FINGER–APOLLO When the Apollo finger is long, its owner will have a love of beauty or lean toward fame and fortune. They will also be cultured, having a fondness for history and the arts. These are loving individuals who delight in helping children progress. If it is overly long, the owner may have a little bit of an ego and be a risk-taker. Although academically clever, they will enjoy money or may even take up gambling.

LITTLE FINGER–MERCURY A long Mercury finger shows a good communicator, whereas a short or stocky finger signals the reverse, making it difficult for the owner to correspond with others socially. If the finger is crooked, the person is secretive. If particularly pointy, you are looking at a psychic type.

Fingernails

The average nail takes twelve weeks to grow from cuticle to tip, so fingernails tell us a lot about the state of health for an individual at the time. The size and shape of the nails can reveal a lot about a person as well. Healthy nails tend to be smooth and supple, with pink skin underneath and a small whitish moon or semicircle at its base. Pockmarks, striations, and cracks are not healthy and indicate something is amiss with that person's health. Additionally, if you see redness in the nail, the owner might suffer from psychological or emotional disorders, often stemming from an addictive nature.

Here's how to read basic nail shapes:

SMALL NAILS These are energetic people generally, but they can have a hot-tempered or impulsive nature. They are pernickety, exacting, and always striving toward perfection. Everything in their home will have a place and a purpose. They possess a witty personality and are often somewhat opinionated. Nails such as these might also tell us that the person is a nervous type or high-strung.

LARGE OR SQUARE NAILS These nails belong to hard-working achievers with a sense of confidence. These people are generally in excellent health, likely to have stamina and determination. They do tend to be stubborn at times and can get fidgety and restless, never sitting still. The owner of these nails can often be prone to minor accidents and could suffer from back problems pertaining to the shoulders and neck areas.

OVAL OR ALMOND NAILS The nicest of all nail shapes, these individuals are kind, friendly, open-hearted, and mild-mannered. They are also open to new people and ideas and will do anything to relieve the stress of others. They shy away from confrontation, preferring to keep the peace at all times. People with these nail shapes are often prone to diabetes or allergies.

WIDE OR FAN-SHAPED These people can hold a nervous disposition and will use up their energy very quickly. They have a daydreamy character and crave stability in life, are loyal to the hilt and thrive on routine. However, they dislike any kind of change and have a strong aversion to criticism.

Reading the Palm Lines

The palm has four main lines: the heart line, head line, life line, and fate line.

Heart Line

This is the prominent line located directly underneath the fingers, running to the edge of the palm under the mercury, or little, finger. The heart line relates to anything representing affairs of the heart, be it emotional health or romantic inclinations. A deep heart line belongs to someone who is creative, artistic, and caring. If the heart line connects with attachment lines, this person will always be the boss in a relationship and have the upper hand. If you see a short heart line, the owner will be very down to earth and single-minded in their approach to relationships. A weak or broken heart line can mean this person has had their heart broken at some point, but this also tells of inconsistency in love or the possibility of unfaithfulness. This person might fall in love with people who are already married or in relationships.

A *chained* line, or a line often intersected by other lines, indicates someone who feels emotions deeply and expresses themselves effectively— maybe a little too effectively at times. The chained line also suggests that this person loves to be in love and is perhaps too free with their heart. Circles on this line mean that the owner will have to take care of their weight, as it could lead to serious health problems later.

Nowadays it is common to see a short twig or fork at the beginning of the heart line, sitting directly below the Saturn, or middle, finger. This indicates divorce or separation from a long-term relationship. If the twig has multiple branches, it would indicate more than one separation.

Head Line

The head line is found underneath the heart line, running across the palm toward the outer edge. This line depicts the person's interest in knowledge and learning. A long head line indicates that the person is not only curious but also perceptive, intelligent, and witty. A short or abbreviated line means that this person has a short attention span and probably has trouble completing projects.

If the head line is merged to the life line, there is a firm attachment to family; this person might stay in the family home, lacking the courage to become independent and leave the nest. When the head line is separate from the life line and a gap forms between the two, the person will be fiercely independent and will probably leave home early in life.

Chains on the head line are not a good sign, communicating that this person can sway toward cluster headaches or general problems with the head. These people may tire quickly, suffer insomnia, or lack energy generally. A break in the head line tells us that the individual will have to beware of accidents.

Life Line

The life line surrounds the base of the thumb in a semicircle. It indicates a person's energy level, their physical health, and how they're doing in the larger scheme of life.

Many people look at the length of the life line to predict how long someone will live. Although that is true to a point, the lines in our hands can grow as we get older, so someone could start out with a short, weak line and go on to possess a much stronger, lengthier line in years to come. The deeper the line, the higher the energy level and the happier the life. If the line is weedy or frail, the owner might suffer from unhappiness.

Look at both hands. It is said that the left hand is what the gods give you and the right hand is what you do with your life. If you are left-handed, this saying is reversed. Therefore, if you are a heavy smoker or drinker, or dabble in drugs, the life line on your opposite hand would be shorter.

If someone has a life line that is interrupted or ends abruptly, that does not mean they are doomed to a short life; it might indicate a tendency toward worry and anxiety. A break in the line can often communicate life changes, such as a brand-new journey or a massive change in circumstance. A deep, red line illustrates a sexy, passionate individual who enjoys a healthy libido.

Fate Line

This line usually runs directly down the center of the hand from the Saturn, or middle, finger to the base of the wrist, although it can go off in different directions. It is a true indicator of character and gives us a great deal of information regarding the owner's destiny. A long, unbroken fate line indicates a person who strives forward in life and has a good work ethic.

If the line travels toward the Jupiter, or index, finger, it shows signs of career success—but often at the expense of a relationship. If it leans more toward Saturn, the middle finger, then the owner will be more successful in life after a time of hard work and effort. Lines that cross the fate line horizontally foretell a difficult life, often troubled with bad luck. Some interpretations see this as more of a spiritual sign, showing that the person is striving for wisdom in life by learning hard lessons.

Mystic Cross

The space between the heart line and head line is called the *quadrangle* and resembles a small runway. If a small cross appears between these two lines, you are looking at someone with a natural psychic ability. This is called a *mystic cross*. A perfect cross will sit directly in the center of the quadrangle without any of its four points touching either the heart or head lines. Imperfect crosses do not mean that the owner is not psychic; rather, they simply imply that the level of psychic ability is not as strong. If you run your finger from the top of the Saturn, or middle, finger down

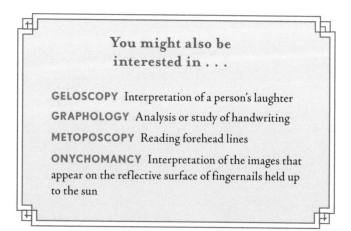

You might also be interested in . . .

GELOSCOPY Interpretation of a person's laughter

GRAPHOLOGY Analysis or study of handwriting

METOPOSCOPY Reading forehead lines

ONYCHOMANCY Interpretation of the images that appear on the reflective surface of fingernails held up to the sun

to the base of your wrist, your finger should pass through this cross. It is quite rare to have one of these, but lots of witches do tend to own one, probably because they take such an interest in the esoteric!

Because the practice of palm reading has worldly roots, there are different interpretations of the same structures of the palm. It's best to learn what you can, practice, and then trust your own instincts. Palm reading is about getting to the root of the person attached to the hand before you. What makes this person tick, and where are they headed? Taking time to quiet your own mind with meditation and an atmosphere conducive to picking up on subtle cues—both physical and the spiritual—are essential to a successful session.

THE SCRYING GAME

Many people picture a crystal ball when they think of scrying, but there are other common forms. To *scry* means to peer or gaze into some sort of surface or medium in order to actually see and interpret images that appear there. Most scryers use a reflective object like a mirror, crystals, a crystal ball, or even a bowl of water. Some people say that the surface itself serves two purposes: firstly to help draw focus away from the distractions of the surrounding world; and secondly to provide a medium for images to come through.

If you have never tried this means of divination, we don't recommend running out and buying a pricey crystal ball right away. Instead begin by using a mirror or a bowl of water.

Create a soothing and relaxing atmosphere that will encourage the universe to work with you. Light a candle and/or incense. Turn off your phone. If you find music helpful, play it on a low volume. Set your reflective surface on a sturdy workspace. Make sure it's at a height where you can look into it comfortably from wherever you are seated. Have a notebook and pen nearby to record your observations once your session is over.

What question are you contemplating? Remember, this is your divination work and you can seek whatever you want. There are no limits. Maybe you want to know if you're going to find a suitable partner in the next year. Or perhaps you'd like to know if you're going to get promoted at work. Then again, you may want to know if you'll be coming into a significant amount of money that is unrelated to work.

Close your eyes. Take several deep breaths, inviting quiet and stillness into your mind. Open your heart to the universe. Allow everything else to fall away.

Now open your eyes and turn your gaze toward your scrying surface. Let your vision unfocus and even go blurry. If you feel yourself slipping into something like a trance, that's okay—go with it. Focus on your question and look at your surface. What do you see? Some of the images may not make sense at first, and that's okay. When you are done, you will have time to decipher what you have seen. For now, just allow the images to appear for as long as they keep coming to you. When the images slow or stop, bring yourself back to full consciousness and start writing about what you observed. No matter how odd or irrelevant it may seem, jot it down. It may be that some of the information is cloudy and confusing right now, but as the days go on, it will become more important to you.

Friends may want you to peer into your scrying surface with their concerns in mind, as well. If you conduct a scrying session for another person, it helps to have an idea of what they want to know, just as you would do for yourself. This is easier than attempting to see the vast, general future. This makes sense: the universe holds an infinite amount of information, so you may get bits and pieces regarding different areas of a person's future, and these may, in turn, be difficult to put together into a cohesive reading.

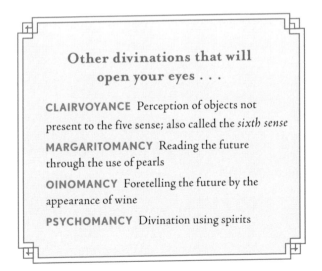

Other divinations that will open your eyes . . .

CLAIRVOYANCE Perception of objects not present to the five sense; also called the *sixth sense*

MARGARITOMANCY Reading the future through the use of pearls

OINOMANCY Foretelling the future by the appearance of wine

PSYCHOMANCY Divination using spirits

A Word About Crystal Balls

Buying a crystal ball is an exercise in research. The first thing to know is that a real crystal ball can be quite expensive . . . and many scrying balls advertised as crystal are actually glass

While it's fine to use a glass ball, a ball made of glass are (or should be) a fraction of the price. You can tell if a ball is made of glass because it will have no imperfections. Zero. Crystal, on the other hand, always has some sort of defect, which is anything but detrimental to its power in revealing the secrets of the universe. A real crystal ball that fits into the palm of your hand can easily cost $50. A glass ball, meanwhile, might cost about a third of that.

Purists say that there is simply no substitute for crystal when scrying. They say it's more powerful and gives better results. It's believed that some crystal balls will know when the right potential owner holds it in their hands and will work to make the connection happen. That is, the ball will speak to the right person and make itself available at the right time for the right price.

My advice is to try a glass ball if you can't afford the real deal. You could even scatter some of smaller crystals around the table as a means of boosting the glass's energy. There are no guarantees on the results you'll get, but it never hurts to combine spiritual forces in this way.

We've only scratched the surface of divination in this chapter. There are entire books written on many forms of divination, so you can dig as deeply as you want to find out more. Get a general sense of what forms of divination appeal to you and go from there.

Chapter 12

Embrace Your Sixth Sense

WITHIN EACH AND EVERY ONE OF US IS A POWER FAR greater than anyone can imagine. This is called a *sixth sense*, and although everybody has it, not everyone knows how to access it. Those people who have mastered the art of tapping into the sixth sense have a natural ability to recognize otherworldly energies around them.

Just like animals, we are all born with a natural ability to detect when a situation feels "off." For example, we rarely see wild animals in the path of a tsunami; they usually sense something is amiss and make for higher ground. This sense of premonition tends to be socialized out of humans, starting from an early age. We have mentioned already in this book how little children (like Leanna, when she was small) can innately identify spirits, primarily because they are not long from the spirit realm and often have a guide close by. For kids, it is natural to state, "I see Grandma on the couch," when Grandma died more than a year ago, but most ordinary families discourage this kind of behavior and put it down to the child being eccentric. Children learn very quickly to suppress these abilities, and over time, because they don't use it, they lose it. Think about a time when you just knew what the outcome of an event would be, without a question in your mind. Whether you acknowledge it or not, you were leaning on your intuition. Most of us have natural skills of premonition, but many ignore these visceral feelings, opting to rely on logic and reasoning instead.

What we are about to share with you next borders on the unknown, the unexpected, and the paranormal. According to our understanding of spiritual teachings, some of us who choose to exercise our psychic gifts have a "call to duty," to try and prevent future cataclysmic events. Sometimes we succeed in changing future events with our predictions. Sometimes we do not.

PREMONITION: SHAWN'S EXPERIENCES

On December 29, 1975, a bomb went off in the TWA terminal, near the baggage claim, at LaGuardia Airport in New York City, killing eleven people and seriously injuring more than seventy-four other innocent souls. Three weeks before the event, I was doing a radio show with a good friend who was a radio host in New York City. The show was about predictions. Both she and I had an avid interest in all matters related to Wicca and the occult. About twenty minutes into the show, a terrifying feeling came over me and I felt my body tense as a vision appeared before my eyes. My friend could sense my discomfort and asked if I was okay. I told her about my vision: I had seen a group of terrorists set a bomb off at LaGuardia Airport. The catastrophe would take place in three weeks. I went on to tell her that many people would be killed or injured.

Sadly, three weeks later my forewarning came to pass. Then, somehow, the FBI found out about my prediction, confiscated the radio tape, and questioned my friend and me as suspects for hours on end. Thank the goddess the FBI agent believed in precognition, and, based upon past predictions of mine that had come true, we were exonerated as suspects in that horrific event. As I have learned throughout my years, fate often warns us, but sometimes destiny is written in the stars.

Years later, I worked in the government-funded CIA Stargate Project. I trained psychics who, like me, had extraordinary extrasensory perception (ESP). We were schooled in the art of remote viewing (seeing people, places, and objects at a distance) in order to spy on the Russians and find hidden Russian submarines during the Cold War. I felt my call to duty had changed from being a prophet of doom to saving the world from harm. In fact, many of the exercises and meditations in this chapter are based on my government training of how to enter the alpha state. The alpha state is a higher, trancelike state of being achieved through the power of the mind, where the sixth sense is enhanced and psychic abilities reach higher awareness. Entering the alpha state was a skill held by many of the mystics of yesteryear.

To me, helping you achieve this ultimate state of being, assisting you in becoming the best you can be, inspiring and empowering you to listen to your intuition and follow your instincts . . . that is my gift to you. I hope to enable you to trust and believe in yourself, open your heart and soul, and use your newfound psychic gifts for the betterment of humankind.

In this chapter, I talk about ways to uncover your extrasensory powers so that you, too, can appreciate the world as you did when you were a child. And I mean *all* of the world, not just the parts that can be seen with the human eye.

EXTRASENSORY EXPERIENCE

ESP, or *extrasensory perception*, is a wide-ranging term often used when talking about a sixth sense. Many other phenomena comprise the sixth sense, too, such as any heightened feelings relating to our other five senses. Some of these are as follows:

CLAIRALIENCE Gleaning psychic information through scents not obvious to others

For example, a psychic who helps with police investigations may smell orange blossoms, indicating that the subjects of a manhunt are hiding out in an orange grove.
Or, more commonly, you may catch a whiff of your long-dead grandfather's cologne or cigar smoke, indicating that he is nearby.

CLAIRAUDIENCE Hearing sounds beyond others' capability

This often includes the voices of deceased loved ones or other sounds that have significance in some way. For example, if someone you know loves the Rolling Stones, you might faintly hear one of their songs while in the same room with this person. Clairaudience is picking up on audial clues given off by the universe or another entity.

CLAIREMPATHY Feeling the emotions or physical sensations of another person

This skill set is very similar to that of an empath, which is a person with the ability to feel the emotions and experiences of others. Most of us can easily sympathize with other people, but clairempathy takes it a step further: clairempaths feel the exact same happiness or pain as another person, or even an animal. People with empathetic powers must be careful not to absorb the energies of everyone around them, as this can be overwhelming and, at times, depressing. Psychics with these abilities must sometimes take time away from other people in order to protect and restore their own energy.

CLAIRVOYANCE Sensing objects, energies, or entities not readily perceivable to others

If you have this ability, you may be able to look at someone and visualize them as a child in the house they grew up in, or perhaps you can see a deceased loved one near another person. You might have a vision of a friend in a situation that hasn't yet happened—in a foreign city, for example, or as a much older person.

MEDIUMSHIP Conversing with spirits

There is a difference between ESP and mediumship. All mediums have ESP, but not all people with ESP can communicate with the deceased and so are not mediums. Some mediums' ability to talk with spirits occurs from childhood; others say they became aware of their skill later in life. Mediums can often see, smell, hear, and feel deceased people and spirits of all forms. People who have true mediumistic gifts are rare. Some profess to have the ability when in fact they might just have a conglomeration of the capabilities listed here. See "Connecting with the Dead" on pages 240–41 for more helpful information.

PRECOGNITION Prophesizing events, or seeing them in dreams, before they happen

Precognitive abilities have similarities to the occurrence of premonitions. People with precognition have predicted global disasters, plane crashes, and even future presidents.

TELEPATHY Reading or sensing another person's thoughts, even over great distances

Twins often possess a reputation for having a psychic bond, knowing how the other is feeling without communicating. This can happen while in the same room or even across states!

It only takes one of these traits to be considered psychic, but some people have more than one and can gather information from multiple domains simultaneously. These are amazing gifts, but if too much information comes in at once, it might also be overpowering. That is why it is so important to take care of yourself and know when you need a break. (To learn about more forms of clairvoyance, read chapter 11, "The Art of Divination.")

Connecting with the Dead

If you feel you might have the gift of mediumship and want to sharpen your senses, it might help to know the following:

The deceased do not hang out in cemeteries. They are usually found in laces that held some meaning for them, like their homes, churches, favorite parks, etc.

It helps to connect with a deceased person if you have an article of clothing or a personal effect of theirs. It is believed that their energy becomes imprinted on these objects, which allows the medium to gain access more easily.

People who die with some sort of unfinished business may be stuck between worlds, which might make it easier for a medium to connect with them. Someone who died without warning may be reluctant to cross over to the next dimension.

Before conducting a medium session, or séance, to connect with the dead, light a white candle and keep sea salt nearby. This will help protect from unwanted spirits entering the environment. Say an opening and closing prayer or statement of protection for the same reason.

Never work with entities that are unknown to you. If you are hearing or sensing a spirit that feels the least bit dangerous, ask them to leave at once and end the session if you must.

Know that some spirits will be confused about where they are and may believe they are still alive. Handling these situations requires a good deal of sensitivity on the part of the medium so as to not agitate an unstable spirit.

You can ask spirits whether they have any messages for their loved ones, especially anyone who is present with you. The spirit may also sing a song that's familiar to their family or show a picture or symbol of something that their loved ones may be able to decipher.

It is vital to remember that all spirits were former humans, and just as there are thousands of personality types in this world, there are as many on the other side. A kind person's spirit will live on in the astral realms, but wicked or vile individuals can also travel to the astral realm and might appear to a medium as a malevolent spirit. Always err on the side of caution and dismiss any spirit you are not comfortable with. It is all right to admit when you see or hear something you don't understand, but if you sense something downright scary, think twice before communicating it to the people around you. Ask yourself if this is necessary and helpful information or if it will cause distress.

PREPARING: SELF AND SPACE

Prior to entering the psychic realm, you need to lay down a little protective groundwork. We are surrounded constantly by positive and negative energies, most of which exist in their own realms. It's important to keep it that way, especially when you start connecting with spirits on other planes.

We are all also surrounded by an aura, an energy field that belongs to us. This highly individualized atmosphere can be positive or negative, as it is a reflection of how we are feeling at the moment of perception. An aura can also act as a spiritual shield when cared for properly. Unfortunately, auras are easily affected by surrounding energies. In other words, if you are in a room with lots of negative people, your aura can absorb that energy and in turn affect your mood. But this only happens if you've inadvertently left an opening for that negative energy to enter.

The best way to secure against negative energies is through good defense, so you'll want to build a strong wall to block yourself and your aura from harm. Think of this as preparation for the emotional strain that psychic work can make on the body. Often, clairvoyants and mediums can experience a slight, dull ache across the bridge of the nose when psychically exhausted, so it is imperative that you recognize this, or any other sign particular to you, and see it as a signal to stop and rejuvenate your energy.

You wouldn't dream of running a marathon without preparing first, right? You must take your preparation for psychic work just as seriously in order to have the most positive experience possible.

A Ritual Bath to Cleanse Your Aura

Your aura is your first line of defense against negative entities, so keeping it in a positive nature and bulletproof, so to speak, is essential. You can cleanse your aura with a simple bath.

Materials

Lavender essential oil, for relaxation and repairing the aura

Citrus essential oil (orange, lime, lemon), for recharging your aura

Bath salts, for detoxifying the mind and body

White candle, scented or unscented

RITUAL

Fill the tub with water that is a comfortable temperature for soaking. Add a handful of bath salts and several drops of both oils. Light the candle and place it where you will be able to see it. Soak in the bath for at least twenty minutes, clearing your mind of any negative thoughts or energy that may you have picked up during the day. Focus on breathing deeply, and imagine inhaling positive energy and forcefully exhaling negative energy. Let your eyes rest on the candle's flame while you envision a white light surrounding and protecting you. Use a washcloth or natural sponge to wash your body.

When your soak is complete, take care to stand in the tub and rinse yourself, either with the shower head or using a large cup and fresh water from the faucet. It's important to wash away any of the negative energy that may have emerged from your body while in the tub.

Dry yourself with a fresh towel and put on clean clothes (not the clothes you were wearing prior to your bath).

Once you're dry, dressed, and comfortable, take another moment to close your eyes and envision that white light of protection all around you—your newly cleansed and invigorated aura. When you feel strong in this vision, blow out the candle.

Crystal Field

You can also recharge and protect your aura by laying out crystals in a particular pattern. Choose from these precious gems:

BLACK TOURMALINE Protects against negative energy

BLOODSTONE Restores energy

CARNELIAN Boosts creative thought

QUARTZ Aids in clearing the mind

ROSE QUARTZ Replaces negative energy with positive energy;
boosts love vibrations

TURQUOISE Aids in healing

AMETHYST, FIRE AGATE, FLUORITE, JET STONE, SMOKY QUARTZ, or any dark-colored stone; protects against and destroys negative energies

Choose at least one protective stone for your crystal field and then choose others based on your specific intention. You can lay the stones on your bed or on your living room or bedroom floor. You can even practice this ritual outside.

Hold on to the stone that reflects the main objective for your psychic connection at this time. For example, if your main goal today is to protect yourself from negative energies, hold an amethyst in your hand. If your goal is to find a creative way to connect with a spirit you haven't been able to speak with in previous psychic sessions, hold on to a carnelian. Lay the rest of the stones out in a pattern or circle that you can rest in the middle of. You can choose to sit in the center of the stones or lie flat.

Focus on your intention for this session. Envision it going just as planned with a successful outcome. When you are finished and feel ready for your reading, gather your crystals. You may employ the crystal used for your main intention (in this case the amethyst or carnelian) during your reading.

When you are finished with your reading, all of the crystals should soak overnight in a salt bath to cleanse them of any negative energy. Afterward set in sunlight or moonlight to recharge.

Smudge Your Space

Before you jump into any kind of psychic session, it's important to make sure the physical space you'll be working in is free from negative energies and entities. You can do this a couple of different ways.

The first method is to gather a bundle of dried sage (easily found at New Age shops or online). Sage has been used for thousands of years to clear spaces of bad energy and prepare them for positive forces.

Materials

Sand, to extinguish the sage after use

A fireproof container or bowl

Water, for safety

Matches or a lighter

A bundle of sage

RITUAL

Fill your bowl with a moderate amount of sand, enough to easily tamp out the lit sage bundle like a cigarette. Have water or a fire extinguisher nearby in case of an emergency. Carefully light the sage over the bowl. You don't want the bundle to have an open flame for your cleansing ritual; blow out any active flame so that the bundle only produces smoke.

Fan the smoke with your hand to waft it around the space where you will be working. Move the bundle of sage up and down the length of your body to cleanse your aura.

As you smudge the area, include a prayer for protection and positive energy:

> *"I call upon the goddess to help cleanse and protect this space and to let in only the brightest of beings. So mote it be."*

You can also make up your own chant or incantation. This is to ensure that only well-meaning spirits or energies can access your space.

Put out the sage in the sand when you are finished. Take a moment to close your eyes and envision a positive connection during your divining session.

Connecting with the Cosmos

Now that you have prepared yourself and your space, how do you go about connecting with spirits or gathering otherworldly information? One way (which might be the simplest for beginners) is by meditating, quieting your mind and freeing yourself from all of the distractions around you so that you can tune into more ethereal signals.

Choose a spot that is quiet and comfortable. Use a fan for white noise if you need to block out environmental noise. Make this space open to a positive energy flow; smudge it if you like, as described in the previous section. Light a candle or incense and dim the lights. If music will not be a distraction, play it at low volume.

Some meditation experts advise that you sit in a comfortable position. Lying flat is also all right, as long as you don't fall asleep. Breathe in as deeply through your nose as you can, and exhale as much as you can through your mouth. Repeat this, slowly, until you feel yourself starting to relax. It may be helpful to count your breaths— four beats in and four beats out, for instance. Focus on your breathing until it is all you are thinking about, continuing with deep inhalations and exhalations.

Now bring your question or goal to mind. Do you want to ask the spirits something? Or are you focusing on connecting with another entity? Allow your mind to travel in whatever direction it wants to go in search of information. Don't focus on whether it feels right or realistic; just continue to relax and go with the universal flow of the moment.

When you slowly bring yourself back to the present, write down your impressions. Were any of your senses heightened? Go through them, one by one: What did you hear, see, feel, taste, smell?

Practice this exercise as often as you can to make yourself more aware of your sixth sense. The more you practice this, the more it will become second nature and the easier it will be to access when you need it quickly.

GIVING A READING

If you decide to perform readings for the general public, here are a few guidelines to follow:

1. **Keep your meetings to no more than one hour per client.**

2. **Try not to do more than three readings in one day.** Overuse of your psychic ability can often make the readings at the end of the day confusing or muddled, not to mention it will leave you exhausted.

3. **If you are female, never read for a strange man alone in your house.** Please understand that this means no disrespect to men, but you must safeguard yourself.) It may be a good idea to have someone else in the home if you do read for strangers in general.

4. **Never try to do a reading if you are tired or unwell;** it can often be a waste of everyone's time.

5. **If you are going to charge money for your readings,** keep your fee in line with other clairvoyants or mediums in the vicinity.

6. **If anyone quibbles about paying for a reading,** remind them that they are paying for your time and that this is your chosen profession.

TEST YOUR PSYCHIC ABILITY

Not everyone wants to use their psychic skills to perform readings or access other realms of existence; some people just want to know the other planes are there. You can put yourself in environments where there's likely to be a lot of spiritual energy—like old houses and antique stores—but you can also work on this skill in the comfort of your own home.

To sharpen your ESP, you'll need a deck of regular playing cards, a notebook, and a pen. Again, you'll want to create a space that's free of distractions and allows you to concentrate on the task at hand. You may also begin with a meditation if you think this will help open your mind.

Take your deck of playing cards and count out ten red cards and ten black cards. At this point, any suit will do. We just want to focus on the colors.

Shuffle the twenty cards well and place them in a single pile.

In your notebook, write the date and make a two-column chart. Label one column **CORRECT** and the other **INCORRECT**.

Starting with the first card in the shuffled deck, predict whether it's black or red. Focus your thoughts prior to revealing the card. What is your intuition telling you? Flip over the card. Was your guess correct or incorrect? Tally each prediction in your notebook. Repeat this exercise with each card in the deck.

When you finish predicting the colors of every card in the deck, you can easily convert your results to a percentage score. (For example, if you managed to get ten predictions right, your intuition is at 50 percent for this practice.)

Practice this exercise each day. Take special note of how you're feeling on days that you do particularly well or on days when you're particularly off. What affects your intuition? Lack of sleep? Hunger? An argument with someone? A great weekend with your family? Knowing this can let you in on when your psychic abilities are at their best and worst!

As you get better at this skill, you can change the exercise up. For example, split the cards into diamonds and hearts and predict which suit you will pull next. You can make this even more challenging by splitting the cards into four groups of five, organized by suit: five diamonds, five hearts, five spades, and five clubs.

If you feel you've mastered this skill (or you've consistently scored above 50 percent), try shuffling the deck and counting out twenty-six random cards and repeat the exercise. This is very challenging but also a great way to test yourself!

Testing Telepathy

We talked about twins being in sync with their thoughts and feelings, but there are many other relationships where this is also true. Mothers can often sense if there is something wrong with their children. Best friends may take on each other's emotions, even on different coasts!

There's a simple way to know if you have a truly telepathic relationship with someone: just ask.

Let's say you talk to your sister every Sunday, and you just hung up from a lovely phone call with her. But by Tuesday morning, you're feeling blue for no discernable reason. You just can't figure it out—nothing sad has happened to you and you aren't feeling sick. In fact, everything in your life is going pretty well. Could it be that your sister is the one having an emotionally tough time right now? You can either make a note of it and ask her during your next phone call, or you might want to give her a call and offer your support in the moment you notice.

If you're truly convinced you have a psychic connection with someone, you two can set up experiments to test the validity of your claim. You might both agree to spend $50 on something very general—a pair of pants or a pair of shoes, for instance. Both of you shop on the same day and then compare your goods later that evening. How similar are your choices?

The ultimate telepathic test involves a pack of Zener cards (available online), which feature a series of rudimentary shapes. If you are in the same room as your telepathic connection, one person can look at the cards while the other draws the shape they are sensing. Over the phone, one person can look at the cards and the other can simply state their guess.

Other Ways to Test Your ESP

Some people like the Zener card test; others want to take their abilities out into the world and hone them. There's nothing wrong with that— no matter how you do it, practice makes perfect. Here are some ways to polish your ESP skills daily:

- **Before you get out of bed in the morning,** take a minute to think about your dreams. Was there anything you might decipher as a message, or as a upcoming good or bad event?

- **While driving to work,** what is your sense that you will find a good parking spot? Can you envision it? Does it feel true? Does it happen? If you take public transportation to work, do you have a sense of when your train or bus will arrive? Will you get a seat?

- **During a conversion,** use your skills of observation and heightened senses. What is your sense of the person you're talking with? Are they genuine or phony? What do you think makes this person tick? What is your empathic sense of this person?

- **Keep track of these experiences**—both positive and negative—weekly if not daily. This will give you a real sense of which type of ESP you are strongest in and which may be better left to others. Maybe you will meet someone strong in an area where you are weak, and you can work together to decipher situations and people.

BE YOUR OWN PSYCHIC THERAPIST

Even if you feel that you don't have one of the ESP traits listed in this chapter, one talent you do have is the psychic ability to read yourself.

How many times have you heard someone say, "If I'd known then what I know now," usually in reference to a choice they made? Sometimes this is a matter of maturity—we make decisions based on a rebellious nature or because we are just too young to appreciate the consequences of our actions. But sometimes we ignore the intuition we're all born with and forge ahead in the wrong direction.

Think about this: more often than not, when things go wrong in a relationship, one of the partners will say, "I should have known. There were so many signs, and I ignored them." After someone has been accused of a terrible crime, people will even say, "There was always something about tem that bothered me . . . but I never knew what." Have you shared similar sentiments? That was you tuning into your intuition, knowing something without concrete information.

Thinking about patterns in your life can be especially helpful in this regard. Are there errors you've made over and over again, like poor financial investments or less-than-stellar choices in partner? It is easy to throw your hands in the air and say, "Well, I just make bad decisions!" or "I have the worst luck!" This might be true, but chances are high that a red flag or two showed itself and you turned a blissful, blind eye.

Thankfully, you can open your mind to intuition and learn to use it more successfully.

- **Start by acknowledging that we all have the skill of intuition.**
- **Learn to quiet your mind as a nightly ritual.** This is akin to meditation, but you don't need to go very deep. Just perform a little review of your day—did anything bother you, anything that somehow didn't feel quite right or (on the other hand) felt great?
- **Take those instances one at a time and explore them.** If you had an odd interaction with someone, examine what, exactly, felt different. Some questions to consider:
  - Was it the way in which they spoke to you?
  - Was there a lack of eye contact?
  - How did this differ from your usual experience interacting with others?

- How did all of this make you feel?

- If you felt uncomfortable, what prompted you to feel that way?

- Likewise, if you felt unnaturally relaxed (around a boss who normally stresses you out, for example), what made you feel that way?

- Most importantly, what do you think was happening with the other person or in the situation?

Sometimes, you're going to know that something "is up" in a situation, but you won't have the exact answer just yet. That's quite all right. Continue listening to your intuition. Ask the questions you need to ask. Push the issue if you can. Take precautions if possible (like safeguarding your money in a financial relationship or getting yourself away from someone who feels like a threat). The important thing is that your antennae is up now, and you won't be blindsided.

If you're interpreting an interaction with another person, then you can also read their subconscious body language to help decipher what's happening.

Read the Body Language

- **Poor eye contact means this person is hiding something**—either good or bad.

- **Turning away from you indicates this person is not open** to the conversation.

- **Standing right in front of you or towering over you is an intimidation tactic.** Someone might do this to convince you their point of view is truth even when you (and they) know it isn't.

- **Crossing arms or legs is not necessarily indicative of anything,** although some people believe this action shows a person is closed-off and has something to hide. However, someone may just be more comfortable in this position.

- **Enlarged pupils indicate stress.** This is sometimes hard to see, but if you suspect your friend is lying and their pupils are large as life, it's a bad sign for them.

- **Perspiration is another stress response,** indicating anxiety or nervousness.

- **Rapid breathing is another sign that someone is uncomfortable.**

- **People who rock back and forth or are jittery while seated are anxious about something.** The same goes for people who bounce their crossed legs or shake their feet while seated.

- **People will generally back away from you if they are being dishonest.** It's a subconscious move that takes them out of your orbit, so to speak, and allows them to feel less guilty about lying to your face.

- **Someone who touches you while they speak to you** (placing a hand on your arm, for example) really wants you to believe them. It's up to you to read their other body language cues and decide whether they are honest.

Take what you felt in your interaction with someone and couple it with their decoded body language. You will, without a doubt, be on the right track. And don't let anyone tell you differently. We are born with this sense so that we can protect ourselves from danger. If something doesn't feel right, that's all you need to know at that moment. It's very important to not only read body language but trust your gut instinct,

especially when it comes to feeling unsafe. If you feel uncomfortable or unsafe in any situation, listen to your instinct and leave. It does not matter if you offend someone—your safety is paramount.

Too often, it's our habit to dismiss out-of-the-ordinary behaviors in someone as them having a bad day. And while we want to give others the benefit of the doubt, we also want to save ourselves from the compounded heartache or headache of knowing something was wrong and failing to act in our own best interest. Women in particular have been socially coded to adhere to principles of politeness—smiling at someone who makes us uncomfortable or being patient and quiet when we clearly want to leave a situation. Do not jeopardize your safety in order to be polite.

Once you hone your ESP, learn to trust your intuition, and make reading into your environment a regular part of your practice, you're going to notice that you make better decisions. This doesn't mean that situations will always turn out the way you want them to, but rather that you don't feel taken advantage of or find yourself on the losing end of matters. Intuition is not quite magick, but it is magickal when used correctly!

EXTERNAL LINKS TO THE SIXTH SENSE

Again, we are all born with five physical senses and this other-worldly perceptive skill, and while this chapter gives much attention to the sixth sense, *all of* our senses are meant to enrich our lives.

For instance, have you ever been in an old house, a historical site, or an antique store and had an uneasy—or very peaceful—feeling come over you? This is a sign that your supersensitive intuition is at work along with your other five senses, letting you know a spirit or some sort of energy is in the area. Those moments are opportunities to tune into your instincts. Even better, they are chances for you to start recognizing whether you can connect through clairvoyance, clairaudience, or other senses.

The next time you find yourself in an environment that seems especially attuned to the afterlife, embrace the opportunity to connect more deeply. Close your eyes and determine what you are experiencing with each of your five senses.

- **What do you smell?** Besides the scents of age, like old books or clothing, do you smell anything more significant?

- **Is there an odd taste in your mouth?**

- **Open your eyes.** Do you see anything out of the ordinary? Shadows, streaks of light, mist?

- **Are you hearing sounds that can't be explained by the surrounding environment**—a voice, laughter, music?

- **How is your environment affecting your body?** Do you have goose bumps? Has there been a sudden drop in temperature?

- **Also take stock of how you feel internally.** Are you queasy? Anxious? Lightheaded?

Strive to open up to that sixth sense now. How do the physical sensations you're experiencing make you feel, emotionally? Are you frightened, curious, or calm?

Checking in with your physical sensations is just as important as paying attention to your sixth sense, so take the time to connect with your body every time you participate in any sort of clairvoyant activity. Visiting historical sites or locations significant to you may be yet another way to sharpen your psychic knack into an area of expertise.

THE PSYCHIC IN YOU

People who can naturally sense spiritual energies and entities do have a finely tuned sixth sense, but just because you don't feel your sixth sense now doesn't mean you can't develop it. The biggest lesson you can take from those with psychic abilities is to be open to spiritual encounters. You must welcome the chance to interact on an ethereal level. The more you allow and encourage these occurrences, the more skilled you will become at automatically feeling the truth of a situation and acting on your instincts—psychic or otherwise.

Clairvoyance in any form is not a skill granted to a select few on this earth—with some practice, you can become completely attuned to your psychic abilities, too. Never doubt yourself. If you have a strong feeling about a situation, person, or event, there is most definitely a reason why, so trust your intuitive side and believe in your emotions. Do this and you are halfway there!

Chapter 13

Psychic Plant Power

FOR THE GARDENERS AND OUTDOORSY TYPES among us, there's nothing more natural than divining through use of plants, herbs, bark, twigs, branches, seeds, or whatever can be found in the wild. Because there are so many types of plants, each with its own magickal energy, there are countless methods for incorporating nature into your psychic readings. This is an ancient practice called *botanomancy*. A book on botany may be helpful if you are identifying plants for the first time.

In addition to talking about how to burn and use greenery and wildflowers to foretell the future, in this chapter we will also discuss modern methods such as aromatherapy to get into the right state of mind for the best reading possible.

BURN AND LEARN

Much of plant divination involves interpreting ashes. Certain plant and herb types were favored in ancient times—sycamore and fig leaves were thought to provide an abundance of good information, for instance—but you can use any leaves you have at hand. You can also use flowers that hold special meaning. Before you gather your flora to burn and interpret, consider these ideas and match them with what you are seeking in your answer:

- Do you have dried flowers left over from a wedding, funeral, or special occasion?

- Might these yield interesting results?

- Is there a special tree, bush, or plant in your yard or that you see often with which you feel especially in tune?

- Have you always felt drawn to a particular fruit or herb?

When divining, consider the meanings and influences of certain flowers:

AMARYLLIS (*Hippaestrum*) Pride

AZALEA (*Rhododendron*) Gratitude

BABY'S-BREATH (*Gypsophila*) Innocence

BUTTERCUP (*Ranunculus L.*) Wealth

CARNATION, PINK (*Dianthus caryophyllus*) Motherly love

CARNATION, RED Passionate love

CARNATION, WHITE Purity and love

DAFFODIL (*Narcissus*) Fresh start

DAISY (*Bellis perennis*) Patience, innocence

IRIS (*Iris*) Good news is coming

LILAC, PURPLE (*Syringa*) Love

LILAC, WHITE Memories

LILY, ORANGE (*Lilium*) Passion (positive or negative)

LILY, WHITE Innocence, purity

LILY OF THE VALLEY (*Convallaria majalis*)
Humility, return of good times

MAGNOLIA (*Magnolia grandiflora*)
Admiration of nature

MORNING GLORY (*Ipomoea*) Unrequited love

NARCISSUS (*Amaryllidaceae*) Loving in vain, ego

ORCHID (*Orchidaceae*) Ethereal beauty

PANSY (*Viola tricolor* var. *hortensis*) Loving thoughts

PEONY (*Paeonia*) Shame, anger, shyness

POPPY, RED (*Papaver somniferum*) Remembrance

POPPY, WHITE Peace

PRIMROSE (*Primula vulgaris*) Eternal adoration

ROSE, PINK (*Rosa*) Youth, friendship

ROSE, RED True love

ROSE, WHITE Innocence

SNOWDROP (*Galanthus*) Hope

SUNFLOWER (*Helianthus*) Purity

SWEET PEA (*Lathyrus odoratus*) Gratefulness

TULIP, RED (*Tulipa*) Eternal love

TULIP, WHITE Pointless love

TULIP, YELLOW Unrequited love

VIOLET, PURPLE (*Viola*) High aspirations or dreams

VIOLET, WHITE Modesty

WISTERIA (*Wisteria*) Homecoming or welcome

The meanings of these particular herbs and other greeneries should also be considered during divination:

BALSAM (*Impatiens*) Passionate love

BAMBOO (*Bambusoideae*) Strength, grace

CLOVE (*Syzygium aromaticum*) True, unending love

CORIANDER (*Coriandrum sativum*) Lust

FENNEL (*Foeniculum vulgare*) Strength

LAUREL (*Laurus nobilis*) Ambition, success

LAVENDER (*Lavandula*) Devotion

MINT (*Mentha*) Suspicion

OAK LEAVES (*Quercus*) Strength

ROSEMARY (*Rosmarinus officinalis*) Remembrance

THISTLE (*Cirsium vulgare*) Beware

WHEAT (*Triticum*) Prosperity

WILLOW (*Salix*) Love denied

Even fruit skins should be considered:

APPLE Temptation, lust, sin, suffering

GRAPE, GRAPEVINE Prosperity, fertility

KIWI Obstacles

MANGO Love, wealth, immortality

ORANGE Joy, prosperity

You can use the petals from a rose, the peel from an apple, a bundle of leaves, or the bark from oak tree—if it will burn, it's fair game! Before you strike the match, however, it's important to set your intention clearly. For example, if you want to know whether your current partner is "the one," then it is appropriate to burn a red rose. If you want to know how your job interview went, burn purple violets. If you're seeking information on whether a loved one will get well from their illness, burn snowdrops.

Whatever you burn, prepare accordingly. Prepare a quiet, peaceful space for your predictions so that you can concentrate on your intention. Like other forms of divination, try to make your question as clear as possible so that you will understand your reading. Consider how your ashy answers will be interpreted. The answer to a question such as "Which of my friends will be at my birthday party?" might be tough to decipher. But a question like "How many people will come to my party?"

or even "Show me what will happen at my party" might be easier to interpret, as they are likely to appear as numbers, a crowd, or some kind of event or activity.

For your items to burn sufficiently, it's important to make sure that any flowers, leaves, or herbs you're going to burn are dried. A moist flower or plant may smolder and affect your results.

The below spell can be used as a guide for your first divining ritual.

A General Spell for Divining with Plants

Materials

Your plant, flower, fruit peel or herb of choice, dried

Fireproof bowl, container, or surface

A lighter and some string or twine

Water, sand, or fire extinguisher, in case of emergencies

RITUAL

Tie up your materials with some twine and place the bundle to be burned into your fireproof container. You may use several different types of materials to ensure a good burn and a readable answer.

Focus on your question. Take a moment to concentrate on what you want to know. Close your eyes and take several deep breaths, allowing your mind to open to the possibility of whatever the answer will be.

Using a lighter, light the bundle. Let it burn to ashes, watching carefully so that the flame doesn't get out of control.

When the leaves, petals, herbs, or fruit skins are ashes, it's time to read. Try not to stir the ashes with your breath or let the wind disturb them. What do you observe? Are there figures, numbers, or patterns in the ashes? Do they represent anything to you? If you're not sure of the general meaning of a particular symbol or figure, do some research on your own to find out.

AROMATHERAPY FOR CLEAR READINGS

In this book, we've talked about how to create a space for manifesting your intentions and visions (see pages 17–19, "Basics of Spellcasting"). Using plant-based essential oils can help accentuate your psychic abilities. Aromatherapy helps open the mind so you can access higher powers of knowledge and vision. Depending on the answers you're seeking or your current energy level, you may want to burn different oils or combinations of them. For example, mint is a stimulating scent, beneficial if your energy is lagging or you're having trouble finding answers to a question you seek. Orange, on the other hand, is a calming scent and may be helpful if you're particularly troubled about a question or topic.

Some oils to try and their uses are as follows:

BALSAM Intuition, grounding, eases stress

BASIL Clears the mind

BAY LEAF Insight, courage

BERGAMOT Calming, encourages optimism

CEDAR Strengthening, soothes anger

CHAMOMILE Acceptance, soothes irritability

CLARY SAGE Grounding, eases fear

CYPRESS Stabilizing, eases loss

EUCALYPTUS Stimulating

GERANIUM Safety and security

GRAPEFRUIT Promotes well-being

LAVENDER Calming, soothes anxiety

LEMON Concentration, stimulant

MINT Clarity, stimulant

ORANGE Calms the mind

ROSEMARY Clarity

SAGE Meditative focus, eases anxiety

SANDALWOOD Bravery

TEA TREE Power, soothes anxiety and stress

VETIVER Grounding, clarity

YLANG-YLANG Optimism, soothes fears

You can use essential oils in several ways. You can put the oils in a bath, for instance, or use with a diffuser (either an electric one or a diffuser that uses a candle under a soapstone bowl). If you are going to use the oils on your skin, you must dilute them first, in a carrier oil like almond or coconut oil. The rule of thumb is 3–5 drops of essential oil per 1 teaspoon of carrier oil. Toss the solution when you are finished, as these preparations can become rancid quickly if not stored properly.

During use, allow the scent to fill your psychic workspace. Focus on your intention and allow your sixth sense to flow freely. Again, you can use oils in combination, so if you are seeking clarity on why you and your beloved recently broke up, for example, then you could try rosemary and cypress together.

DIVINING THROUGH FRUIT AND SEED

You can also use various fruits to divine the future. We talked about apple peels in the section on superstition (page 128), but here's another way to get an answer from this common snack: Hold the apple by the stem with one hand while twisting it with the other hand. Recite the alphabet. The stem will come off the apple when you get to the letter of the first name of your true love. You can also use the apple seeds for this purpose. (You will need a candle in a container or a fire.) Assign the name of a possible love match to each of the seeds and toss them, one by one, into the flame. The seed that makes the loudest popping sound indicates the name of your future mate.

You can do something similar with watermelon seeds, by again assigning a love interest's name to each seed, then sticking each seed to your forehead. The one that falls off last is to be your future one and only.

Daisy petals are another way to know whether someone loves you. We've all done this one: Think of your love interest and then pick each petal off a daisy one at a time, saying, *"They love me, they love me not."* Continue until you've taken off all of the petals. The last petal will tell you if this a dream romance or a fly-by-night relationship!

Here's a little project that can help manifest an answer to a question with multiple possible answers: Take a handful of seeds and several small flower pots. Label each pot with a possible answer or outcome. Plant seeds in each pot, all the while focusing on your intention or question. Care for each pot of seeds in exactly the same way. The pot that sprouts first (or, in the case of sprouts appearing at the same time, the pot that grows strongest) is your answer. You can try this outside, too, of course, especially if you're seeking an answer that has the potential to change over time!

Bay Watch

Bay leaves are especially useful in predicting the future, as they can be used in several ways. If you have a group of people present and you want to know, for example, who is going to get married first or who will have the most successful new year, then use the same number of bay leaves as there are people present. With a pencil, mark one bay leaf with a dot or *X* on the back. Put the leaves in a pile, faceup, and have another friend write everyone's names on the leaves, as this person will have no idea which leaf has been marked. Now place the leaves in a bowl and have everyone choose one leaf.

The leaf with the mark on its back indicates the person who will get married first or have good fortune!

You can also give extra energy to your wishes by using bay leaves. Write your various dreams on several bay leaves and place them in a bowl to burn. This is supposed to underscore your intentions, by sending them into the universe for manifestation! Bay leaves can also be burned during meditation or scrying to enhance your metaphysical visions. *Dream pillows*, or pillows stuffed with bay leaves, can be used to augment visualizations as well.

PLANTS FOR SPELLS

Practitioners of magick take matters into their own hands by using brews and spells to bring their desires to fruition. Certain plants provide protection, boost your individual power, or enhance visions. You can start gathering some of these materials on your next walk in the outdoors. Of course, if you want to have an abundance of some of these plants, flowers, and herbs for use in your readings, you can plant your own psychic garden—a good idea if you're starting to do a lot of psychic work or if you are providing insights for friends and family!

ALOE (*Aloe vera*) Protects against evil spirits and mishaps at home

ANISE (*Pimpinella anisum*) Keeps nightmares away if placed in a pillow or sachet; keeps dark energies away when used during spellcasting or meditation

BASIL (*Ocimum basilicum*) Useful in love spells

BLACKBERRY (*Rubus*) Ensures good health and wards off evil spirits; also helps manifest money and success

BLACK COHOSH (*Actaea racemosa*) Another plant used in love spells; also promotes self-esteem, self-reliance, and self-assurance

BLOODROOT (*Sanguinaria*) and **CATNIP** (*Nepeta cataria*) Both attract love, peace, and positive energy; place on your nightstand with rose quartz.

CHAMOMILE (*Matricaria chamomilla*) Brings money into your life and draws abundance in other areas of your life as well. Can also remove negative energies by soaking in it.

COWSLIP (*Primula veris*) Used in healing meditations and spells

ELDERBERRY (*Sambucus*) Promotes prosperity and removes negative energies; put it around your home—over doorways, on tables, or on your mantel—or carry a sprig with you

FENNEL (*Foeniculum vulgare*) Protects against dark energies; usually hung in windows and doorways or grown in the yard

HIBISCUS (*Hibiscus rosa-sinensis*) Brings love and abundance; useful in love spells

HOLLY (*Ilex*) Another plant used for protection from negative energies; also used in love spells and potions

LAVENDER (*Lavandula*) Useful in love spells—use lavender oil on your clothes or skin to attract someone into your life

MARIGOLD (*Tagetes*) Protects from negative energies and unwanted visitors; plant around the yard or keep inside your home

MINT (*Mentha*) Attracts success; protects from unwanted energies; draws positive spirits when used in a meditation or spell

NETTLE (*Urtica dioica*) Removes negative energies or reverses a curse; also used in healing

OAK (*Quercus*) Twigs and acorns, placed in and around the home, protect from storms, particularly lightning and floods

ROSE (*Rosa*) Popular for love spells; also attracts peace and well-being

Although you can find many time-tested spells in books and on the Internet, you can create your own spell or potion depending on your intention. **Before you create a potion of any sort, however, make sure the herb or plant you're using is safe for human ingestion!** Something like chamomile or mint is safe, of course, so let's say your intention is to have a more positive attitude and attract good things and people into your life. Opening up your meditative space while drinking a cup of mint tea is the perfect way to bring this about in your life. Sip the tea while you envision letting go of old sorrows and regrets, picturing the life and people you want. You can even chant an incantation if you want, something like,

> *"I picture the life that is to be, Spirits, please bring it to me."*

You can also make a potion or tea from blackberries while envisioning great success. Let's say you're an artist and you want to sell several of your pieces this year. Picture your artwork in great detail, imagine the person who will buy each piece, and envision the money you will receive in exchange. If you are looking for financial success in any sense of the term, you might use an incantation like,

> *"Money comes this way so free,*
> *This I know and this I see."*

A Spell to Find the Ideal Mate

Materials

> Bloodroot or catnip, for attracting love
>
> Rose quartz, for boosting love vibrations
>
> A pink or red candle, for love, and candle holder

RITUAL

Take the bloodroot or catnip and place on your nightstand with rose quartz. Light the candle, and focus your intention: either the one you love or the ideal mate for yourself. Concentrate on who this mystery person. What might they look like, how tall might they be, do they have a sense of humor, are they quiet or boisterous? Picture the person coming into your life and the two of you having a successful relationship. This should take 5–10 minutes. Snuff out the candles.

Another Spell to Find a Mate

Holly can be used in a similar love spell.

Materials

> A sprig of holly, for love
>
> Rose quartz, for boosting love vibrations
>
> 2 pink candles, for love
>
> A pink rose, for love
>
> A glass of water

RITUAL

Place the holly, rose quartz, and candles on a clean
table or surface. Light the candles and pluck the
rose petals, placing them around the holly sprig, rose
quartz, and candles while you envision your perfect
mate or focus on the object of your affection if they are
already known to you. After 5–10 minutes, drink a full glass of water
and snuff out the candles.

A Spell for Illness

Materials

> A bunch of nettle
>
> A medium bowl

RITUAL

Nettle can be used when someone is ill. Place a bowl of nettle under the
sick bed (or couch) where the person is trying to recuperate and focus on
their getting well. Do this for several minutes, envisioning the person in their
formerly healthy state. Leave the nettle under the bed or sofa.

Appendix

WITCHCRAFT FAQS

Finding your greatness comes from knowledge, and we believe that this is where magick happens. Only then can you create your own destiny and find your personal path. Everything evolves over time, and nothing more so than witchcraft. There are some Wiccans today who still follow the traditional pagan beliefs, but most have embraced modern methods and adapted traditions to suit their own practice.

We believe it's not just by happenstance that our book found its way into your home, and we can only hope that it finds its way into your heart, also. Everything happens for a reason; maybe the universe guided you here to learn and become the next future generations of leaders, teaching and helping others learn the craft. In order to help you on your journey and because, having read our books, you may still have a few queries, we have put together this section of frequently asked questions.

LEANNA AND SHAWN
ANSWER YOUR QUESTIONS

Q: **Is Wicca and witchcraft the same thing?**

A: This is a much-talked-about topic of conversation. From a historical point of view, Wicca is one type of witchcraft with roots in paganism. It is deep-set with spiritual beliefs that honor the gods, goddesses, and angels. Witchcraft steers more toward the practice of magick and spellcasting, and there are people the world over that practice the craft without being Wiccan. There is a slight difference between the two, but nowadays many refer to witches as being Wiccan.

Q: **Is Wicca a feminist faith?**

A: Most religions hold at their center a strong male deity, a father figure who presides over the universe. Of course, the patriarch is different from faith to faith—some are gentle, others are more heavy-handed—but he is always male. Wicca is different in that it celebrates the divine feminine as well as the masculine—the god and the goddess. This acknowledges that the female sex is every bit as strong, resilient, and creative as the male. In fact, one sect of Wiccan faith, Dianic Wicca, honors only

female goddesses, so yes, it's fair to say that Wicca appears to lean toward being more of a feminine following, but there are also many men who practice Wicca.

Q: **Do all Wiccans practice their faith the same way?**

A: Not even remotely! Just as there are many sects of Christianity, the Wiccan faith takes many forms, including angelic, shamanic, faery, circle craft, eclectic, Gardnerian, Dianic, celtic, and British traditionalist. Each offshoot differs in its rituals, population, symbology, beliefs, and in various other ways. Having said that, most groups have some beliefs in common, including an intimate relationship with nature and basing many of their practices on the cycles found in nature. (Read more about the different forms of Wicca on pages 8–10.)

Q: **What is Angelic Wicca?**

A: Angels have been present in magickal practices for centuries, but the term angelic Wicca has become more popular over the past thirty years or so. This modern movement of witches tends not to follow the teachings of the god and goddess but prefers to serve the angelic vibration instead.

Q: Is Wicca a cult?

A: No, Wicca is not a cult. Cults tend to have an earthly leader who is shown devotion by the cult members. Wicca is a spiritual movement in which supporters practice freely and often in a solitary manner. They worship only spiritual deities and regard every living thing on the planet as equal.

Q: What part does sex play in witchcraft, and do witches perform ritual orgies?

A: Sex is celebrated by witches because it is part of nature, and Wiccan couples who have chosen to be together might, in fact, decide to participate in sexual rituals privately. Tantric sex is often a favorite. Generally speaking, very few if any ritualistic orgies take place in Wiccan society today. Witches see intimacy as a very special act that bonds two loving individuals together. It is not something a witch would do with just anyone or in a public place.

Q: Do you use blood sacrifices in your spells?

A: The life force is valued greatly, be it that of a tiny ant, a beautiful tree, animals in the wild, or a human being. In ancient times, blood sacrifices did take place as it was seen as a way to honor the gods. As Wicca has become more sophisticated over the centuries, these sacrifices have virtually ceased to exist, and so you will not usually find Wiccans participating in such rituals. The faith is much lighter these days, with more onus put on the well-being of all living creatures.

Q: Do witches worship Satan?

A: No, witches do not believe in Satan, as he stems from a Christian concept and most Wiccans do not ordinarily believe in Christianity. Satanism and witchcraft have two completely different followings. What they do have in common are some of the symbols, with one being the pentagram. History tells us that during the early onset of Christianity, Christians did adopt many, if not most, of the pagan sabbats and symbols. During the reign of Roman emperor Constantine the Great from 307–37AD, the first antipagan laws came into play. Temples were burned to the ground, and Christian followers vandalized and tore down pagan monuments. Christians wanted to reign supreme so the horned god, Pan—an icon of reverence for the Pagans—was denounced as the Devil, and those thought to be practicing paganism were referred to as Devil worshippers. They met a grizzly end. Many ancient pagans converted to Christianity to save their own lives. Satanists, who worship the fallen angel

Lucifer, use the pagan symbol of a pentacle in the upturned position, which represents their Devil, but for Wiccans the pentacle still signifies the original horned god, Pan.

Q: What is the difference between white and black magick or good and bad witches?

A: White magick is practiced with the best of intentions and with a positive energy. White magick comprises rituals and spells performed for the greater good, including through healing, prayer, and love. Black magick has a much darker intent—these are spells and rituals used to inflict harm or set darkness into motion. Placing a curse on someone is an example of practicing black magick. Today a person is not considered Wiccan if they practice the dark arts. Some even go so far as saying there is no such thing as a white witch; they simply use the term witch instead, negating the possibility that black magick even exists. Their argument is that witches cannot be dark, because a true witch only works with positive magick.

Q: I think someone put a spell on me. How can I tell if I am cursed?

A: One very important fact to remember is that you can only be cursed if you believe it. Now, if someone tells you they have cursed you, it may be hard not to believe it, especially if things start to go wrong in your life. Curses thrive on fear and create a massive ball of negative energy that clings to a person. This, in turn, starts to give you a feeling that someone has hexed you. To counteract any curse, place tiny mirrors, facing outward, in every window in your home, and meditate, picturing yourself in a golden globe of light.

Q: What is the difference between a wizard and a warlock?

A: In the most general terms, the terms warlock and wizard are used interchangeably to indicate a male who practices witchcraft. However, there are some variants in how the words are used by some groups. Wizard is used to describe a male who is very wise and uses his magick judiciously, while warlock is used to designate someone with a darker energy and malicious intentions.

Q: Can I be Christian and Wiccan?

A: While the leaders of Christianity would most likely disagree, this is really up to you and your comfort level in blending two separate beliefs, each of which have their own tenets. The Bible states that there is one god and followers shall not worship any other gods. Wicca is polytheistic, meaning it celebrates multiple gods and goddesses; this flies in the face of the Christian belief system. This is not to say that Christian Wiccans do not exist—indeed they do. These men and women have simply found their own personal way to meld two belief systems. But, generally speaking, Wiccans won't care if you're Christian. Christian leaders, on the other hand, will almost definitely frown upon practicing Wicca.

Q: Are all Wiccans witches?

A: Remember this difference: Wicca is a spiritual following, while witchcraft is a practice. Witches engage in magick by casting spells, creating potions, and the like. Not all witches are Wiccan. In theory you could belong to any number of religions, or none at all, and still practice witchcraft. Likewise, not all Wiccans indulge in witchcraft. Many choose to concentrate on their spirituality and worshipping the divine without venturing into magick of any kind.

Q: How do I know if I am a witch?

A: Contrary to myth, witches are not wart-ridden hags who fly on broomsticks and wear pointy hats. They are simply people who have a love for Earth and nature and believe in a divine essence, whether that be god, goddess, angel, or nature. A true witch does usually have an interest in all things magickal and will possess a fascination for most esoteric subjects. We believe there are millions of witchy types out there who do not even recognize the fact that they are witches. Often the person will know from a young age that they are different from others. They might have a fascination with the moon, have a deep belief in magick, or like to use or grow herbs and plants. You have to delve into your psyche and follow your heart. If something in these pages rings true to your soul, you are probably a natural witch.

Q: It is thought that one of my ancestors was a Salem witch. Does this make me a witch?

A: If you have a personal pull toward witchcraft, it could be that you are a hereditary witch (see "Which Witch Are You?," pages 8-10). Often if someone has a knack for witchcraft in their genes, they may develop a fascination for all things pertaining to the craft from an early age.

Q: Sometimes I predict future events. Does this make me a witch?

A: Not necessarily. Not all clairvoyants are witches. It is true, though, that witches can be proficient in the art of divination, mainly because they have an interest in it.

Q: What is a Wiccan initiation?

A: When a person has been practicing Wicca for some time, they often choose to take part in a Wiccan initiation, which

The Evil Eye

This is a type of curse that anyone can unintentionally cast upon someone else without even realizing it. The power of the mind is dominant within all of us. Sometimes, simply thinking badly toward a person can create a negative ball of energy, which in turn manifests into an unlucky force directed at the receiver. You have to be very careful not to send out hatred to another person, as this negativity can cling to them. If the recipient discards the negative vibe, it will travel straight back to its initial source (you) and engulf the sender in the same bad luck. This is why witches believe that what you send out, you can invariably get back. It's best to always keep your thoughts neutral. If you are feeling particularly angry with someone, walk away and distract your mind with something else.

is a dedication to follow the Wiccan path. Think of it as the counterpart to other religions, such as the Christian tradition of a baptism. In this case, the person is given over to the gods and goddesses and devotes themselves to this spiritual path. The initiation is usually conducted by a coven's high priest or priestess and involves passing power from an elder to a new initiate. Those who want to practice in a solitary way may embark upon self-initiation. This is usually done during a new moon phase, to represent the soul being born into a new faith. There are various self-initiation rituals, such as the one on pages 288–89.

Q: What is the Wiccan Rede?

A: The Rede is a lengthy proclamation of the intents and tenets of witchcraft. It's a moral guide for practicing magick. The short form follows:

"Bide the Wiccan Law ye must,
In perfect love, in perfect trust,
Eight words the Wiccan Rede fulfill:
'An ye harm none, do as ye will.'
And ever mind the Rule of Three:
What ye send out, comes back to thee.
Follow this with mind and heart,
And merry ye meet, and merry ye part."

There is a much longer form of this that you can find with a simple Internet search, but this passage gives you the idea.

The overarching theme of the Rede is to do no harm when practicing magick. Many witches read through the entire statement prior to engaging in spellcraft. Some like to display the Rede on a wall in their home.

Q: If I follow Wicca, will I attract evil spirits?

A: In a word, no. Wicca gets a bad rap in some circles, seen as a means of worshipping dark forces or connecting with evil entities. In truth Wicca celebrates many aspects of nature as well as the divine masculine and feminine in all of us. There are many Wiccan rituals that one can practice, but as in all things, your intention sets the tone. If you mean to call on a malevolent entity, you'll be sure to attract one sooner or later. But if your intention is to connect with the sacred god or goddess within you, then your experience will be one of positivity and peace.

Q: What is a witch's circle, and why is it important?

A: Prior to practicing a magickal ritual, witches sometimes cast a circle. This is done by drawing energy into the circle, to define the sacred space and/or for protection from negative energies and sources. The circle can be cast visually—that is, simply by looking at the area you wish to signify—

or you can create a field by drawing a circle in chalk or salt, or by placing four symbols of the elements in the four directions of your circle. (North is for earth; South is for fire; East is for air; West is for water.) You can also set a candle at each of the cardinal points. Some traditions believe the circle has to be nine feet in diameter, while others believe the size of the circle should be left up to the witch to determine based on the purpose of the ritual to be performed. You can also include other elements in your circle—again, based on your intention. If you're casting a love spell, for instance, include some rose petals. For prosperity, coins or precious stones may be used. If you are working with a coven, all members should stand inside the circle and focus on the same intention, raising the collective energy inside of it.

Q: How do I set up my altar?

A: Firstly, if you are more inclined to follow tradition, it is important to decide in which direction you want the altar to face. East-facing is preferred by many, probably because the sun rises in the east, but it is really up to you and to what you feel drawn. A table or work surface will suffice; modern witches have even been known to use the work tops in the kitchen. You can adorn your altar with a cloth if you wish, or if it's made of wood, you might like to leave it bare and celebrate its beauty.

Other items you might want to add to your altar are:

- A statue of your chosen deity
- Large altar candles positioned toward the back of the altar
- Totem animals, such as hares, cats, and owls
- A chalice, seashells, and mirrors, to represent the water element
- Objects such as stones, pebbles, leaves, bones, or the pentagram, to embody the earth
- Feathers, to symbolize your angels
- Certain crystals, appropriate for whatever task you have at hand
- Flowers or petals relating to the spell you want to perform

Q: What is a Book of Shadows?

A: This is a diary of sorts for a witch—it's where they keeps rituals, spells, notes on herbs, crystals, candles, and the earth's elements, or anything at all that will help improve their practice. Some like to begin a fresh journal annually, starting it by writing in the lunar calendar for that particular year. Dreams are written in the book, and any spells that were tried and tested are also recorded. The Wiccan Rede may also be included to help set the intention before each ritual. Witches take great pride in this book, sketching and writing various incantations, poems, prayers, and other texts. There may also be a Book of Shadows kept by the high priest or priestess of a coven, for use when the coven is gathered together. Traditionally, the Book of Shadows is destroyed upon a witch's death, but nowadays they are passed down to family members or other likeminded witches.

Q: Do witches really fly on broomsticks?

A: According to legend, witches would use hallucinogenic herbs such as henbane, nightshade, and mandrake root as "flying ointments." These were thought to be applied to the genitals by using the staff of a broom and would make a person feel like they were flying. However, they were highly toxic and could even cause death.

The Wiccan term for a broomstick is besom, and today many witches will have one propped up by the hearth to use in house cleansing rituals. They will sweep the floor toward the doors to rid their homes of negative energy. It is thought that the staff of the besom represents the male genitalia, and the brush the female genital area, symbolizing both the masculine and the feminine.

Q: Do I have to use candles in spells?

A: The simple answer to this question is no. Not all spells require a candle. Experienced Wiccans would even go so far as simply visualizing a candle burning while reciting their incantation. If you do use candles, it is important to make sure that you are using the correct candle color for your spell. If you are ever in doubt about which color is appropriate, you can use a white candle; this is neutral and will work for anything.

Q: How do I increase the magick within me?

A: When a person is new to applying magick, it may feel as though you're just going through the motions, waiting for something to connect. Well, you're half right. It is all about connecting with the forces in the universe, and there are ways to enhance that relationship. Meditation is particularly useful, especially if you quietly sit somewhere outside. Because Wiccans have a special relationship to the earth, they can draw energy from the great outdoors simply by being in a natural environment. You can expand the magick within by practicing spellcasting more and more. It's a bit like going to the gym and working your muscles; the longer you stick with it, the more proficient you become. You can also increase your abilities by simply reading lots of literature on the subject.

Q: How do I know if I am meditating properly?

A: When you are completely relaxed and meditating properly, you will feel as light as a feather and very floaty. If you can maintain this state of meditation without falling asleep, you will benefit from it significantly. It is also thought that ten minutes of proper meditation is the equivalent of four hours' sleep. Sometimes you might see visions appear behind your closed eyes or experience the feeling of your spirit rocking back and forth.

Q: Where can I buy the supplies I need for my rituals?

A: For the most part, you will be able to find everything you need either in a New Age shop or online. The Internet has made practicing the craft a breeze. No more searching up and down for wolfsbane and eye of newt—add it to your online cart and have it shipped! (Also, online shops can easily tell you what can be substituted in place of ancient ingredients.) One of the most wonderful things about being a twenty-first century witch is that we can now access tools and herbs from all over the world. Once upon a time these were virtually impossible to get, whereas now we can get the exact items we need to perform a spell.

Q: Isn't it wrong to cast spells for money?

A: Witches today believe that money is just an energy necessary for survival on this planet. There is thought to be a universal pot of money that we can all draw on every now and again when the need arises. It is doubtful that, when casting spells for cash, you will get a huge amount for your efforts; often we just receive what we truly need. If you cast a spell to win the lottery or come upon a vast sum of money, you will be sadly disappointed at the result. Make sure your need is genuine; only then will you be able to pull from that universal pot.

Q: Is it safe to cast a love spell?

A: Yes, it is, as long as you use your common sense. Within most Wiccan communities today, it is not ethical to cast a spell that might interfere with another person's free will. However, in some ancient folk magick it was quite natural to cast spells for love. Think about the consequences of such actions and how it might affect you further down the road. Casting spells to draw love to you is probably a better, safer idea, rather than spelling for a certain individual to fall head over heels for you. Other alternatives are to use magick to make yourself more attractive to others or to become more confident in yourself.

It is quite safe to weave magick to heal rifts in relationships, make a marriage happier, and to move on after relationships have ended.

Q: What is a handfasting?

A: A handfasting is a Wiccan betrothal ceremony initially founded in western Europe. Most couples like to perform this during a new moon phase. It was originally a temporary marriage or engagement, committing a couple together for a year and a day. After this period of time, exactly one year and a day later, the couple would then renew their vows to seal the marriage permanently. The service is usually performed by a high priest or high priestess, and the couple tie the knot by having their hands bound together with colorful ribbons (see page 287).

Nowadays the bride and groom will invite guests to the occasion and, in place of bringing gifts, the visitors will produce plates of delicious foods and some fine wine, which is then shared among all the people present. If the weather permits, the ceremony can take place outdoors, or for those who live in rainy climates, an indoor event is more appropriate.

Q: What is a Wiccaning/ Naming Day?

A: A Wiccaning or naming ceremony is a Wiccan alternative to a child's baptism and is usually a joyful occasion. The baby is welcomed into the Wiccan faith and a ritual is performed to bring safety and protection to the child. The celebrations are similar to that of a handfasting, where guests bring food offerings. A gift created by the guest is usually also included, representing good health, prosperity, and happiness for the child. Often the ceremony is performed outdoors, with the guests forming a circle around the mother, father, and child. If the weather is bad, a more informal affair can take place within the home. A godparent, sometimes known as a godsfather or goddessmother, is an allocated member of the circle, chosen to help and guide the child in the faith through the course of their life. They is also invited into the circle as the high priest or high priestess conducts the service. The child is then officially given a name, and celebrations follow.

Q: Can children cast spells or is this dangerous?

A: For those who dedicate their life to Wicca, it comes naturally that they should want to teach their children the ways of the craft. Children can be introduced from an early age. Because no one advocates children playing with fire, they may only practice noncandle magick until there are old enough. The earlier a child learns about their gods, goddesses, guides, and angels, the more chance they will have in connecting with them as they mature.

Q: Do I have to believe in magick for it to work?

A: Casting spells successfully means that you need to project positive intent. The more you believe in the fact that your spell will work, the more effective it is likely to be. If you doubt your own ability, it is unlikely that the spell will work.

Q: Is it safe to use a Ouija™ board?

A: You do have to be careful when playing with the Ouija. Some experienced witches see it more as a divining tool, whereas others believe you can inadvertently allow malevolent spirits to cross over into the earth plane.

Q: Is it okay to pay for a spell online and have someone else cast it for you?

A: Spells cast by the individual for their own needs are far more likely to work than those performed by someone you don't know. Sadly, there are many charlatans out there who might take advantage of those new to the craft, so with this in mind, we do not recommend anyone paying for a magickal act. However, if you know someone who is gifted in the art of spellcasting, you might like to request a spell and make a small donation toward the cost of candles, oils, or other materials that might be used.

Q: How can I find other people that are like-minded and interested in Wicca?

A: It is still quite difficult to find established covens, whichever area you live in. Nowadays witches are using technology to their advantage and joining online Wiccan communities. This is a great idea for widening your knowledge on the subject, as you will come across many different cultures and will also be able to share spells and rituals with all kinds of people.

Q: How do I tell my family I am a witch?

A: This question gets asked a lot. There is still a stigma associated with the craft, but this prejudice only stems from ignorance. The best way to break someone in gently may be to tell them what you are reading and then hand them The Witch's Way when you have finished it.

ROLES AND OFFERINGS
IN A MODERN HANDFASTING

High Priest or High Priestess This is a coven's male or female leader experienced in Wiccan practices. He or she will lead the ceremony and unite the couple in matrimony.

Right-Hand Man The old phrase describing the best man, this is a brother or friend close to the groom. He will ring a bell before the ceremony begins, calling the gathering together. He will tend to all the groom's needs during the day.

Handmaiden Today we refer to this role as that of a bridesmaid. The bride can have as many handmaidens as she chooses. These ladies perform an important role in the ceremony, fetching and carrying the objects from the altar to the high priest/ess throughout the service.

Altar Maiden This woman prepares and looks after the altar throughout the ceremony.

Salt The salt is brought to the high priest/ess by a handmaiden and is scattered at the feet of the couple to purify and cleanse them.

Ritual Food Many blessings take place during a handfasting. Bread and wine are a symbol of fruitfulness and ensures that the couple will always receive enough food to thrive. The couple will drink the wine from the same ornate chalice and eat a small piece of bread. A basket of bread and a cup of wine is then taken by the handmaiden to all of the guests to share and rejoice.

The Honey Blessing takes place before the couple makes their vows to each other. The vows are usually written by each individual and spoken after the high priest/ess touches their mouth with the back of a spoon laced with honey.

Feather, Oil, and Ribbons The altar maiden hands the high priest/ess the feather, who then dips it into the oil to anoint the wrists of the couple. The altar maiden then passes the ribbons on a cushion to the high priest/ess, who then binds their hands together. The couple then presents the hand binding to their guests.

Wedding Bands Like a traditional Christian service, the couple exchange rings, which are worn on the third finger of the left hand. It was believed in ancient times that a vein ran directly from this finger to the heart.

Broomstick After the blessing, a decorated broomstick is placed on the ground and the couple will hold hands and jump over it. This custom comes from the term "living over the brush."

Self-Initiation Ritual

Materials

Tall white candle

1 (26-ounce) container of salt

Pentagram jewelry

Ritual

To begin, you will need to choose a Wiccan name.

If you are lucky enough to belong to a coven, it is a nice gesture for a member of the congregation to choose a magickal name for you. If you are not part of such a group, meditate on a name that you connect with and ask your guides to give you a sign. You will know when you have chosen the right name for yourself, because you will love it and feel a deep connection with it.

Take a warm bath. Afterward dress in something loose-fitting. Try to be as free from earthly restrictions as possible, and make sure the house is quiet.

Light a tall, white candle and stand inside a circle of salt. Speak these words:

*"I, {say your Wiccan name}, wish to know
the mysteries of the universe and honor the gods,
goddesses, and angels.*

*I will seek to gain knowledge and wisdom in the craft
and always follow the Wiccan Rede: to harm none.*

*I am willing and able to uphold the laws and principles of Wicca.
Today I am born anew, as a child of the gods, goddesses,
and angels. I will walk with them beside me.*

*I ask you now to guide me on my new journey so that I may grow
closer to you and understand the wisdom you send me.*

May my mind be blessed so that I can accept the wisdom of the divine essence.

*May my eyes be blessed so that I may see my way clearly
as I embark on my new path.*

May my lips be blessed so that I may always speak with respect and honor.

May my heart be blessed so that I can love and be loved.

May my hands be blessed so that I can use them to heal and help others.

*May my feet be blessed so that I might walk beside the gods,
goddesses, and angels.*

I hereby pledge my dedication to the craft.

So mote it be."

After you have spoken your troth, wear your pentagram jewelry
as a symbol of your initiation. You can let the candle burn for a few
hours before blowing it out. You might like to relight it in the future
when you perform spells, or you can save it as a memento.

Afterword

WITCHCRAFT TOMORROW
The Hope, the Vision, the Dream

LEANNA GREENAWAY

In one way or another, I have spent the past twenty-eight years trying to dispel the awful myths about witchcraft and attempting to bring the truth to the surface regarding this gentle faith. For me, a world in which the craft is not considered to be a dark art is my ultimate wish. I would love to see more witches across the world forming covens of their own, guiding and teaching other like-minded people about the wonders of witchcraft. My dream is to see Wicca worshipped universally with ease and to finally have its place back in our modern world.

Deep down I believe that all things magickal will escalate with today's younger generation. I get hundreds of letters each year from teenagers and young adults alike, eager to learn more about Wicca. Many speak of the craft as having a ring of truth to it; they feel compelled to learn more and ask questions. It gladdens my heart and leaves me delighted to find so many taking an interest.

You don't have to be a Wiccan to invite something spiritual into your life on a daily basis. Place a few crystals around the home, play meditative music regularly, and surround yourself with beautiful objects. If you are thinking of embarking on this wonderful journey and embracing the hidden witch within yourself, always strive to do good. There is so much hatred and unhappiness in this world, and if you can make a difference to just one person in your life, then you have done your job. It really is healing for the soul. My spirit guide Peter told me that we must strive to be better, for that is our main purpose in life. So be kind to others, and try to be patient, especially with those who haven't caught up with you yet. Remember, everyone is on their own path, going along at their own pace.

SHAWN ROBBINS

It is my fervent prayer that the students of today become the teachers of tomorrow. We live in a world of great opportunities, surrounded by love and magick. Yet those purer virtues are in danger if we forget our roots and heritage. This much is clear: we must fulfill our responsibilities as witches, because we are much stronger together than apart. We should endeavor to safeguard the riches of our planet. The real heroes are those who rise up and speak out. Show kindness and understanding to those less fortunate in life, and stand up to the social and religious injustices that threaten our very existence. Above all, we must prevail by leaving behind a legacy filled with gratitude for those who walked before us, those whose writings and teachings lead us into the future. The well-being of our craft springs from the growth of our collective knowledge and wisdom, which will be passed on to others. Our history has already demonstrated that we will prevail. What I hope for you, and for all of my sisters and brothers everywhere, is to know that you don't stand alone. We are united as one.

Acknowledgments

$\mathcal{A}$T STERLING, THE MAGIC BEGINS HERE. We
would like to thank our brilliant editor, Barbara Berger, for
harnessing the power of the pen, and bringing *The Witch's
Way* to life. And to our agent, Bill Gladstone, at Waterside
Productions, we raise a cup of tea to thank you for your belief
in two witchlings whose books are the gateway to knowledge.

Also at Sterling, we are also grateful to cover art director
Elizabeth Lindy for the beautiful cover design; Sharon Jacobs
for the brilliant interior design conception, direction, and
production; production editor Michael Cea; and production
manager Terence Campo. We also thank designer Barbara
Balch for assisting with the lovely layouts.

INDEX

PICTURE CREDITS

Clipart.com
243, 247

ClipArt Etc/FCIT
146, 270

Depositphotos
© Julia Faranchuk: 51; © nafanya1710
(chamomile): 267

Courtesy Dover Publications
96, 142, 149, 155, 158

Getty Images
Paul Art: 6; Awispa: 81; Natalia Barashkova: 44
(unicorn); Bauhaus1000: endpaper B, 33, 79;
Benoitb: viii (woman), 101, 214; Bokasana: 59;
Channarongsds: 147, 237, 238, 264; Cjp: 99;
Clu: 29; Cofeee: 132; CSA Images: 77, 201, 232;
Curly Beard (sword): ix, 20, 30; The Dafkish: 147,
129; Duncan1890: 38, 109, 225; Epine Art: 57,
267 (orange); Gameover2012: 208, 254; Geraria:
65, 66, 67,163, 267 (dropper); iarti (rays): xiii;
Ilbusca: 123 (shooting star), 125, 131, 165; iStock
Collection: 128; Itskatjas 244–45; Hpkalyani:
14; Jonny Jim: endpaper C, 45, 75, 256; Jpa199:
117, 166; Kentarcajuan: 106; Macrovector:
112; Man_Half-tube: 23, 116, 144; Marabird
(butterfly): iii, vii, 15, 39; Maystra: 130 (mirror),
162, 249; Constance McGuire: 36; Mecaleha: 68,
262 (daffodil), 268; Nastasic: 40, 218, 220; natrot
(rays): 82–90; Nicoolay: 9 (broom), 13, 74, 222;
Andrii-Oliinyk: 263 (sunflower); Paprika: 137
(angel); George Peters: 34, 212, 246, 259; Valeriya
Pichugina: 52; Pimpay: 41, 50, 54, 62, 63, 71,
72, 127 (ladybug), 262 (orchid), 263 (bamboo);
Pleshko74: 274; Polygraphus: 42; Den PotisevT: 56,
203; Powerofforever: 229; Raveler1116: 207; Olga
Rom (color pentacles): 83, 85, 86, 87, 88, 89, 90;
RonyGraphics: 130 (keys), 250; Irina Stankevich:
102; Stdemi: 153 (hand); Nataliia Taranenko: 47;
Top Vectors: 271; traveler1116: 206; Vladayoung:
18 (compass), 169, 288, 306 (sun and moon);
whitemay: 124; ZU_09: 198, 211, 292

National Gallery of Art
35

Rijksmuseum
Endpaper B

Shutterstock
Agsandrew: 139; Appolinaria: 140; artnLera
(rosemary): 267; Artur Balytskyi: 170, 172, 174,
178, 180, , 186 (archer), 188, 190, 192 (fish);
Marijus Auruskevicius: 293; Eugene Dudar (broom,
pentacle): front cover, i, v, xiv, 92, 194, 283; Geraria:
133, 266; Istry Istry: 27; Ka Li: 176, 182, 184
(scorpion); Kuzmicheva: 105; Shlpak Liliya: 49;
Alina Maksimova: 269; Anne Mathiasz (triple
goddess glyph): xii, 134, 138, 150, 216, 233, 239,
274; Aleks Melnik: 272; Moopsi: 280; Morphart
Creation: 111; Nafanya241: 24; Drug Naroda
(zodiac glyphs): 171, 173, 175, 177, 178, 181, 183,
184, 186, 189, 191, 192; Hein Nouwens: 22, 78;
OK-SANA (leaves, front cover and throughout);
Pio3 (cat): iv, 5, 302; Perunika (cat): front cover,
spine; Vera Petruk (key, vine and pentacle border):
306; Renikca: 8; Manekina Serafima: 119; Transia
Design (feather): front cover, spine; Tukkki: 241

Courtesy Wellcome Images
157

Courtesy Wikimedia Commons
Endpaper D; spider: v, 4; 9 (nettle), 12, 31, 43,
44 (Green Man); butterfly: 100, 109; 126, 199,
205, 209, 215, 217; bird: 3, 60, 95, 197, 235, 261;
Pearson Scott Foresman (owl): 127, 288

Courtesy Yale University
xiii (four elements)

NOTES

NOTES